Not Afraid to Live with Dandelions

Everything Has Purpose

Judy Williamson

La Pointe Press

La
Pointe
Press

Published by La Pointe Press

P O Box 16063

Elway Station

St. Paul, MN 55116

Book Design by Cory Barton

Barton Design

4140 Vincent Avenue South

Minneapolis, MN 55410

Library of Congress Control Number 2004090239

ISBN 0-9748685-0-7

Printed in the United States of America

Dedicated to life's vast array of teachers—

my absolute favorites being Mom, Jill, Michael, Matthew,

Jinah, and Stacey.

Introduction

Lucky, my golden retriever, and I walk daily. On one particularly cold, dark, and icy Minnesota morning, Lucky was pulling mercilessly. Gentle commands and corrections with the leash did not dissuade him from the relentless tugging. I began to slip. "Halt!" I commanded. To the amazement of us both, he did. I regained my footing and reached to scratch behind his ears. I was ever so grateful that he had obeyed and wanted him to know it. "Lucky boy," I playfully suggested, "if I fall and break a leg, we won't be able to walk for weeks. It is in your best interest to take good care of me."

As I spoke those words I realized that I had routinely assumed that those I loved were looking out for my best interests—as I was trying to look out for theirs. How often had I counted on someone else to meet my needs? The question did not need an answer; simply by raising it I discovered an explanation for many of the disappointments in my life.

Can I control what happens to me? Hardly, and I am not sure that I want to. I have found the situations I work hardest to prevent are often the wisest of teachers if and when they do occur. Lucky and I have taken two series of obedience classes and worked with a personal trainer in an effort to make him a more predictable companion. It hasn't happened yet. It apparently is not what I need at this time. I can't begin to guess what he might do, so to avoid difficult situations I must be vigilant. Because of Lucky's presence, my awareness of all that is around me is heightened, a gift when I choose to see it that way.

It is pointless to be frustrated or angry with him; he is giving me what he has to give. Regardless of what is happening, there is a blessing waiting to be discovered if I have the patience and the desire to look for it. The unexpected turns, or tugs in this case, provide an opportunity to see the lessons that life has to offer. I believe there is something to be gained from every situation. When I am willing to accept the gift being given, I can then embrace the teacher, whomever, or whatever, it may be. When I'm not, I've noticed that the lesson has a tendency to sprout anew, often with greater strength.

Teachers are disguised in the common, the ordinary, not unlike a dandelion growing in the yard. A dandelion can be viewed in a variety of ways—as can all things. Choice allows me to admire the simple flower with its radiant sun-like color, offer a freshly picked bouquet to a special someone, make a salad of the tender spring greens, or see it as a blight in a lawn that I believe should be weed-free. My perspective matters not if I understand that it is merely a reflection of my relationship with myself. Past experiences, emotions, and expectations all have an effect on how I see what is before me. Knowing that, my reaction to the dandelion becomes a mirror that is reflecting something of what I believe about myself at that very moment. It is simply a teacher, and a precious one, as is my furry friend.

We all have choice in how we act and feel, and in this particular situation I chose to laugh. How naïve my assumption had been that others were looking out for me, and how grateful I was for the awareness that they were not—a beautiful gift presented to me by my four-legged wild child, and amazingly, I got it! What fun it was to be alive in that moment.

The sun was just beginning to peek over the horizon when Lucky and I arrived home. What a wonder-filled day it had already been. As I opened the door, I knew that my perspective would be forever different and that each moment of each new day also holds the same promise of awareness, and with that, the joy that fills body and soul. *Thank you, Lucky!*

What We Need
Isn't Necessarily
What We Want

Susan died in 1991. She was a very special friend. We lived life on the same page. Our kids were similar in age. They went to the same schools and participated in many of the same activities. We even attended the same church. Our paths crossed often, so we shared our days and our common course.

Being generous of spirit, Susan gave freely with joy and a sense of humor that softened the obstacles, the obstinate, and the ornery. She was a second mom to my kids and a safe place for me to turn when life seemed overwhelming.

Our adventures were filled with surprise and wonder. Together we made fun, and quite often mischievous, we had fun. We were connected in spirit, she supporting mine and I hers, and we felt blessed to be sharing time and space.

A few years prior to her passing, Susan had routine back surgery on a problematic disc. The following morning I went to the hospital to be with her while our husbands navigated the soccer schedule with our combined families of seven kids. I entered her room expecting to see her ever-smiling face.

"Good morning," I said as I approached her bed. "How are you feeling?"

"I'm feeling fine, but I need to ask you a favor. Please promise that you will never leave me alone in a hospital," was her surprising reply.

Without having to think, I assured her that I would be there for her if a need arose. I wondered what had prompted her to make the request; her surgery had gone very well. Our lives were overflowing with the busyness of our families, working, and enjoying what life had to offer. Being sick or injured was just not a part of the equation. She of all people didn't have the time or desire for it. What was she thinking?

Susan's recovery was blessedly uneventful. She barely skipped a beat, and we marched on. We thought we would do so forever, but life had another plan. My husband changed jobs. He was given a wonderful opportunity, but it necessitated that we move to my hometown, St. Paul, Minnesota. The blessings were mixed as we left behind the many friends and places in Des Moines that had been our center for fifteen years and returned to a much loved city and the newness that had been created by my long absence. Life was pregnant with possibilities, and I was able to keep one foot in both of the worlds I loved, building a new life in our new home and visiting the old just 250 miles away.

The visits became more frequent when, within months of our moving, Susan was diagnosed with cancer. The doctor believed it to be very manageable. Remission was not only possible but highly probable. We did not speak of death. No one imagined that this was a life that could be stilled. Susan was fully alive. Not even the chemo was able to keep her down, nor did it eradicate the disease in her body.

One dreary December afternoon I was folding laundry. There was a football game on in the distant background. The kids were tackling homework in the upper reaches of the house. It was quiet. When the phone rang, I sprang to answer it, looking for a respite from sorting out the mountain of socks that was patiently waiting to be paired. It was Susan's father-in-law. "Susan isn't expected to make it through the night," he told me.

I wondered how that could possibly be. Ten days earlier Susan and her husband, Jim, had traveled to an East Coast cancer center for a new procedure that was designed to enhance the effectiveness of a coming treatment. Susan was hoping that it might actually be a vacation. She would be treated as an outpatient. There would be no hospital gowns, no IVs, and no tasteless meals. In between appointments, she was planning to stroll along the waterfront with her special guy and feast on fresh seafood.

"What happened?" I asked.

"No one really knows. She went into a coma last night and was admitted to the hospital."

There were several phone conversations between Jim, his family, and me. We were in agreement that someone should be with Jim and Susan. For various reasons none of their family members were able to travel, so I was on the next plane. I had three long, undisturbed hours to think about my promise to stay with her if she were hospitalized. I thought about the what and the why of it. I felt like an actor in a play. I had not written the lines or designed the set, but I had committed to playing a supporting role to my dear friend. How the script was to end was still in question, but I thought I knew who might be producing and directing. We were in loving hands, I felt safe, and it seemed that in spite of the unknowns, there was nothing to fear. How strange that I was so calm; this clearly fit my definition of a crisis. I simply knew that what was needed was presence, and I had been asked three years earlier to pledge mine. The stage was set.

She did make it through that night—and many more. I came and went, balancing the schedule of her family with the needs of mine. Ever mindful of the promise I had made, my loyalties were divided. I never imagined that I would have to live up to my promise and certainly had no plans for how to proceed. Life had been turned upside down, but for some reason, nothing felt out of place.

It took weeks for the doctors to figure out what may have happened, and they were very uncertain as to what the future would hold. They suggested that she might be in a coma for a long time, so one cloudy January day, I decided to go home to be with my family.

I had packed that morning and planned to leave after visiting with Susan at the hospital, but there was a different plan brewing. We were buried by a snowstorm that the forecasters hadn't seen coming. Travel was out of the question. Nothing was moving with any measure of safety. Susan and I often laughed and joked about how I am so capable of missing life's subtle, and sometimes very obvious, clues, but the storm was a sign that even I could not fail to notice. The entire region was covered in a blanket of deep, heavy snow, and I was given no option but to remain true to my word. I had to stay put. There was no decision to make and nothing to juggle or balance. I felt at peace as I settled in for another night at the hospital with my beloved friend.

Night times in hospitals are eerily quiet. The emptiness is punctuated by the beeping of the machines that support life—Susan was attached to a plethora of monitors and medical devices by a tangle of wires and tubes. I was feeling uncomfortable in the silence that seemed to separate us. Normally, we shared everything. I wanted to speak with her; I wanted to connect with the spirit that I knew to be alive and vibrant within her unresponsive body, so I dared her to join me in a game. I asked her a question, selected a machine, and then asked her to make the numbers on that machine increase by two if the answer was yes. I was curious to see if anything would happen. Many things did. Numbers bounced merrily up and down and lights flashed, always the exact amount and on the precise machine I had requested, as she answered my questions.

"Susan, do you know where you are?"

"Do you understand what is happening to your body?"

"Susan, do you know that your kids have been here?"

"Have you seen your mom sitting by your side?"

"Do you feel Jim's presence as he tenderly rubs your feet?"

We talked for as long as I could think of questions to ask. I didn't want to let go, so miraculous was it to me that we were communicating. We were connecting. We were connected through the power of spirit. That we were living in different levels of consciousness didn't matter. That night was one of the most amazing, and at the same time the most heartbreaking, of my life. We both knew that her body was unable to recover. Part of me was alive with the joyous wonders of life. The rest of me was numbed by the changes that were upon us.

Thanks to the force of Mother Nature, the next morning I was by her side, holding her hand, when Susan passed to the next circle of life. She was at peace, and in an odd way, so was I. Nothing that had happened in the last month made much sense, but I knew that there was purpose in all that had occurred. There just had to be. I had been forewarned three years earlier that this time would come. We were supposed to be in this place, at this time, together, and miraculously, we were.

The promise I had made was that I would be present, and presence was what I was able to give. Without having awareness of what I was doing, I spent that month living in the moment. I was focused on what was, the here and now. There was little point in letting my mind drift into the past. Looking for explanations or reasons for the change in Susan's physical condition wouldn't change a thing. Projecting into the future was too unsettling; I didn't want to think about life without her. I didn't worry about my family when I was away. I knew they were doing just fine without me, so I was able to keep my attention on the needs of Susan and her family. When I was at home, I was busy catching up on the normal day-to-day activities and preparing for the holidays. I spoke with Jim almost daily and then just had to let go. There were many things that I needed to do. In that month, wherever I was at the moment, I simply had to attend to what was before me, a true blessing.

In the big picture, this was a situation with many labels. Horrible, heartbreaking, unbelievable, and devastating are some that come to mind, but in each moment, it was a sheet that needed to be changed, a hand that needed to be held, or a feeling wanting to be shared. In each moment, we were all okay, and it felt very peaceful. Eckhart Tolle has written a book about that magical space between the past and the future. It is called *The Power of Now*. Living in the now is amazing. It makes it possible for us to do extraordinary things, particularly in an emergency, when we are so focused on what is immediately before us that we prevent unrelated distractions from creeping in.

I did not understand how I had arrived at such peace, but I did know that I had been given a taste of how life could be, regardless of the situation I was in. Surprisingly, the opportunity grew out of a situation that, by my definition, should be void of such.

I had played my part to the end, the bittersweet end that was so very confusing. I was feeling fortunate to have walked by Susan's side and to have shared in her journey. I also was exhausted, sad, and in disbelief that we had lost her physical presence. My mind went looking for answers and sought definition for what had happened. I found only *what's* and *why's*. I bounced between the past and the future and lost the power of being in the now.

I had honored the commitment made, and thinking my job finished I returned home. After an eleven-day absence, one clear priority was the laundry, or maybe that was just all that I could handle at the time. Regardless, I began sorting the whites from the colors, the *to bleach* and the *not to bleach*, and the questions that bubbled up through the pain.

What We Have Isn't Necessarily What We Need

$\mathcal{At}$ the time of Susan's death I was forty-four years old, the mother of four beautiful, healthy children, and the wife of a successful businessman. We lived on a quiet, tree-lined street in a graceful older home that promised to be warm and inviting as soon as the renovation was complete. The hectic pace of juggling the children's activities, volunteering, tiling bathrooms, and keeping up with the laundry was balanced by our coming together every evening for a family dinner. It was our time to connect and share with each other. It appeared that I had it all, so why was it suddenly so difficult to get out of bed every morning?

Grief was an undeniable companion. I missed my pal. More accurately, I missed knowing that she was there when I needed someone I trusted. Our regular contact had been changed by the move to St. Paul, but knowing I could find her if need be bridged the gap. I felt her in spirit, but that didn't feel like enough.

I was at a loss for words, for the ability to shape my day, or for finding joy in the tasks before me. The air had been completely blown out of my tires. I needed time to stand still so that I could get my bearings, but time refused to comply with my wishes. It marched on. There were lunches to be packed, carpools to be driven, walls that were desperate for a new coat of paint, and a family that counted on me to maintain some semblance of order. I let those needs take priority over the ache in my heart. I tried to maintain a sense of normalcy that I just didn't feel; it seemed to be better for everyone else.

One of Susan's many special skills had been as an aerobics instructor. It seemed natural to join an aerobics class, putting what energy I could muster into my health and fitness. It was something that I could do for myself while honoring her spirit. I knew that my friend would want me to let go of the pain and live life to the fullest. She certainly had, but it was not to be for me, at least in the short term. Within a few weeks, I was experiencing severe lower back pain. The results of an MRI were normal. Thankful as I was that there was no identifiable injury, it also meant that there was no pill or medical treatment that could offer instant relief.

The prescribed treatment was rest. Was the doctor kidding? I was assured that he was not and was told to stay off my feet. I complied as best I could. Lying down did provide relief from the physical pain, but it seemed like an incredible waste of time. It was spring break. We had visitors from Des Moines, and the weather was perfect for doing yard work. I wanted to be anywhere but lying down. I was being too resistant to see that there was a point. I needed time to grieve and process and had not had the wisdom to give it to myself. The universe does provide, however, and it did. It was my job to recognize the opportunity given and be open to it. As yet, I was seeing no opportunity within the confines of my situation. Instead, I was struggling.

Up to that point, I had not regularly given myself much of anything. I believed others' lives and needs were far more important than my own. I could do for myself tomorrow or next week. I hadn't noticed that tomorrow never came. In the busyness of providing for others I ignored my self. Actually, I didn't know that there was a self separate from the daughter, mom, wife, and friend that I was to others. The discomfort in my back made doing for others out of the question no matter how much I wanted to. I was miserable, completely and totally miserable, and wishing for a magic wand that could wave it all away.

One morning after seeing the family off to work and school, I crawled back in bed, as was my habit of late, and for a diversion turned on the TV. My sister-in-law called. "Hi, what are you doing?" she asked.

There was no faking it; not one ounce of perky was left in my pathetic body. I didn't have the energy to hide the truth. "I'm lying in bed watching Geraldo."

We both burst out laughing. It was nine o'clock in the morning, and I was lying in bed watching someone else live his life instead of living my own. This was not the road to relief from the ache in my back and the ache in my heart that I was desperately wanting. What was I doing? Something needed to change, but what? More questions wanting answers. I hadn't a clue where to find them.

In complete disgust, I reached for the remote and turned off the television. Maybe peace and quiet would bring clarity. I began to think about what I would change if anything were possible. My first impulse was to look at others. Life would be better if so-and-so would only....

The list took on a life of its own. I wanted the kids to take more responsibility for household tasks, and I wanted my husband's support in making it happen. I wanted simple requests to be honored the first or second time I made them so that I didn't have to resort to nagging. I was tired, and I was tired of expressing a need or a desire or a belief and being completely dismissed or ignored. I felt invisible. I felt invisible to the very people I loved.

Are others responsible for how we feel? At the moment it seemed to be so. I was angry.

As a matter of fact, I was furious. I was angry that Susan had died, I was angry that no one volunteered to do the laundry or load the dishwasher, I was angry that my body was rebelling, and I was angry that I was angry. I was also angry that no one was rushing to my side to provide support and comfort. That, however, proved to be a blessing in disguise. In my many hours of solitude, I began to mull over two recurring questions. How had I come to this place of such discomfort with my life and with myself? Why was I feeling such anger? I didn't know.

What I did know was that I had felt the presence of anger more often since we had moved. Starting over had clearly been more stressful than I had recognized. I'm sure that the stress was exacerbated by the feelings of loss connected to the passing of my dear friend and of my father's passing just three months earlier. Regardless, I was way out of balance. It was time to switch the focus from others to myself.

True, at the moment, day-to-day living would have been easier if others had chosen to help with the daily tasks, but the real issue wasn't what others were or were not doing but what I was doing to myself or not doing for myself. Each journey begins with a single step; I had now discovered a direction to take, and I was ready and willing to move forward, even if not completely able. Tomorrow was going to be a better day; I was going to make it so. I just didn't know how. I called on an old friend, dogged determination. It had often served me well.

Gingerly, I stepped back into life. Resting had helped. Being on my feet was still painful but becoming less so. Emotionally I felt drained. That seemed like an improvement as well. I was still too close to see purpose in the last few weeks of pain, but I had identified something to fix. The anger had to go. It was destructive to me and, more importantly, to my family. We were all deserving of better.

Gary Zukav, the author of *Seat of the Soul*, says that anger is a form of fear. I agree, and I also see it as a creation of our ego, the mind searching for an identity. Fear is born in projection, the *what if's* and *maybe's* that live in the future, a time that doesn't actually exist, and fueled by the disappointments and events of the past that we have allowed to define us. We invite it in when we perceive change as a loss, and I was doing just that. My mind was eager to dig up old grievances or fly into second-guessing what the future might bring. I was living anywhere but in the moment.

My heart was searching for peace. I did not know where to find the road that would lead me back to the peace I had known when I was at Susan's side, but I knew it was there. So I did the only thing I knew to do. I took another small step forward and changed just one thing. I began to pay attention to my feelings and the situations that triggered them.

Doing that proved to be a powerful tool that slowly moved me from automatic pilot to making thoughtful choices and observations. When I felt frustration or anger creeping in, I would try to step back, even if only for a second, before I responded. By witnessing the feelings rather than being caught up in them, I was then able to deal with the situation calmly. The drama of an emotional reaction was no longer necessary when I was able to differentiate between the situation and how I felt about it. When the ego, our self-image, is not involved, fear doesn't exist, nor do problems. It is then easier to deal with the situation as it is—in that moment.

The kids, just by virtue of being kids, were extremely generous in providing opportunities for practice. "Everyone else is going." "I'm old enough to do what I want." The beauty of teenage teachers! I don't know that I was wise enough to thank them at the time.

I am awed by the perfection of timing. By virtue of the kids' ages and stages, they too were searching for clues to their individual identities and trying to sort out emotions. In many ways we were on the same path, though I believed mine to have the additional responsibility of providing security and stability for theirs. We had more in common than our roles would suggest; the ground was ripe for building, and so we did. I invited the family to come along for the ride. What could we learn together? The possibilities seemed endless. This was likely to be a glorious adventure and all the more so if shared.

Little by little my sense of humor returned, and the days became brighter. Not too surprisingly, the pain in my back began to lessen as well. Exactly what was the connection between emotional and physical pain? Another interesting question to add to the growing list. I was feeling impatient that there appeared to be so few answers.

There are a few words that begin with the letter *p* that I have never really liked, *process* being one of them. It suggests that there is an order to things, specific steps to take, and time needed for completion. *Patience* is another of my least favorite words. Had anyone asked, I would have requested a quick fix, please. No one did. Another *p* word, *pattern*, is closely related to *habit*. Quite possibly, this was an area that I needed to seriously address. It appeared that changing my life was going to take time and a concerted effort.

I was surrounded by people I loved but feeling very alone. I wasn't though. There was support all around me. It came simply in the magnificence of a spring day or gentle words of encouragement, often by complete strangers, and was always offered at the perfect moment. Quietly, I was being led to a greater awareness of spirit and all that is available to us. Two old friends in particular helped me along the way. I didn't have names for them then, but I now know them as *faith* and *intention*.

We Are Given
What We Need

The knowing that things will work out is what I now call faith. At the time, I was not aware of its vastness and power. I trusted in an all-powerful presence, but it posed more questions than it gave answers. There were too many unexplained wonders and happenings for me to deny the existence of God, but at times it seemed that loving, universal power was nowhere to be found. I couldn't name it or define it, but I had a knowing that all was well even when it didn't appear so. I had experienced that sense of knowing in the plane as I flew to be with Susan and in the peace I felt as I sat by her side. Thinking back, I remember feeling it many times. I certainly responded differently to life when I was in that space. I wanted more. I wanted to live in the quiet, peaceful place of knowing. I wanted to live more in the moment and less in the chaos and drama. Trusting in a universal presence gave me the courage to continue to move forward. My sense of determination gave me the tool.

For as long as I can remember I have been able to clearly define goals and just go for them. Defeat is not in my vocabulary. Turning away from a sticky situation is at best temporary and most often just not an option for me. *Mind over matter* is my motto. Holding the intention is the first step in creating the reality; I know that with every ounce of my being.

By determining to make changes, I set wheels into motion to do just that. Even without awareness of all the love and support that the universe was providing, I was calling it in by my desire to change, and it came. I believe it comes for all of us. The challenge is learning to see the answers that are presented and recognize the gifts being given.

One of the gifts was a very part-time job. I worked for a company that organized incentive travel and business meetings for other corporations. My responsibilities were to travel with the participants and serve as a facilitator for their event. I was always working outside my immediate comfort zone: a strange city, a foreign country, a new hotel, or maybe even a new client. The only constant was the unexpected. The days were long, and the challenges were many, but I loved it.

Packing my bags and leaving the family behind to pursue something that seemed frivolous, because it had nothing to do with my *real* life, didn't fit my definition of what this mother should do. It was difficult for me to tear myself from the role of parenting. I take parenting very seriously, but I also had been taking responsibility for things that were not mine to be responsible for. The family was used to my being present and I was used to picking up the pieces, but misplaced books and forgotten homework did not really need to fall into my realm. I was searching to find balance between supporting and enabling, guiding and controlling. I wanted to foster an air of independence in each of us, and in so doing, create a space for myself. There were times when I felt guilty about being away for a week or ten days, so I filled the refrigerator and the cookie jar with favorites and prayed that my absence was as good for them as it was for me.

As I checked in for my flight, I would enter a vastly different world. Regardless of the challenges of the pending assignment, a shortage of hotel rooms, lost luggage, or changes made at the eleventh hour, it was easy compared to the challenges of parenting my wonderfully creative teenagers. I often joked that I was the only person I knew who called working eighteen-hour days a vacation, and it truly was.

Rarely did the job allow for leisure time in the beautiful cities, countries, and hotels where I worked. It did, however, provide simple gifts like a hotel maid to pick up my towel if I was in a hurry, meals cooked by someone else, and a room that was mine, all mine. It didn't take much to make me blissfully happy, and I relished these simple pleasures for years before I learned to look beyond them and discover the real gift I was being given.

When I was working, I was a member of a professional staff, a working partner. Apart from my usual roles, I was seen as an individual, something I had lost sight of. Repeatedly I heard people thank me for being patient in a difficult situation. That always surprised me; at home I was seldom acknowledged for such. At work

I was appreciated for being a team player and honoring others. Amazing! At home I tried to create an environment of cooperation, but teamwork was rare, often requiring more pleading and nagging than it was worth. Somehow, our lack of togetherness felt as if it were my fault.

I often found myself believing that I was inadequate or wrong, making it difficult to accept words of support and appreciation. Instead of receiving a compliment I was quick to say, "Thank you, but...." I believed in my abilities, but I didn't believe in my self or my worthiness.

The gift being offered was a clearer picture of who I truly am, the essence of me that was hidden within and absorbed by the roles I had willingly assumed. I wasn't entirely ready to see myself in that light, and no one looking from the outside in would have guessed that I didn't know myself apart from my roles.

Thankfully, when we miss an opportunity to grow, we are always given another and another and another until we are ready to see what is before us. Sometimes, it takes a miracle. In 1995 I met an angel.

That spring, one of my children was having a particularly rough go of it. Behavior had changed drastically, and moods were swinging. I did not question the need to cancel the programs I had been assigned for work. Nothing could ever be more important than one of my fledglings. Within days I had a safety net encircling my floundering child. Everyone at school knew to call me if something was amiss, counseling began, and boundaries were strictly set so that contact with a new, and to me frightening, peer group was limited. A psychologist and a well-intentioned friend suggested that I let up. They believed I was too restrictive and likely to cause more rebellion. Regardless, I stood firm in my resolve and the boundaries remained.

A couple of weeks after I had battened down the hatches, I no longer wanted to deal with life as it was for another moment. I went to bed at eight o'clock one night, literally pulling the covers over my head. I was begging for mercy when there was a knock on my door. There was something that needed to be said. Would I listen? Frankly, I didn't want to. I had closed the door purposely so that I would be left alone. I had had enough, and I said so. I heard the door open. Reluctantly I peeled the covers back from one eye as this loving voice said, "This is going to sound strange coming from a fifteen year old, but thank you for loving me enough to keep me safe when I wasn't being loving to myself. I wish my friends' parents were paying as much attention."

I was overwhelmed by the courage behind those words and through my tears could only respond with a simple, "Thank you." I was warmed by the love and honesty expressed and grateful for the wisdom and protection that had been given to us both. It was definitely a moment worth staying home for.

I had not been expecting that things would work out as they had. We were truly blessed. By grounding my troubled teen, we both were given the gift of time spent in solitude. It was time that I used to sort out my priorities. Once I had a direction, I was then able to act out of love, love for us both, rather than react out of fear. First and foremost, I didn't want my child to be hurt. Secondly, I didn't want to live with the chaos of a teenager spinning out of control.

I used intuition as my guide, another old friend, that soothing voice of wisdom that comes from within. It had always been there, present as far back as I can remember, but as in this situation, it so rarely jibed with what others were doing or saying that it was often just too difficult to honor. This time, there was too much at stake. I didn't feel I had a choice. I followed my inner voice, hoping the naysayers were wrong. Safety was the issue. We would just have to deal with the opinions of others later.

Later never came. Within a few seemingly very long weeks, my child and I had moved to a greater understanding of each other and ourselves. There was no need for criticism or judgment, ours or anyone else's. Believing in and following that gentle voice within led me to make decisions and create boundaries with love.

In hindsight the solution appears to have been so simple. It wasn't.

I often doubted myself. *What if's* and *should's* and *could's* churned in the already muddy waters. As best I could, I chose to deal with what was and let the future unfold in its own sweet time. I sought solace and solitude in my garden, a place of connection, where my mind is quieted and the wisdom of silence can be heard. I needed to listen with care for the guidance, which was gentle, loving, and perfect in every way. As we made it over each hurdle, trusting my intuition became easier. Believing in the voice within was imperative. Living in the moment was essential. And always, practice and patience, two of those pesky *p* words, were key.

I was so focused on trying to follow my inner voice that it took weeks for me to realize a miracle had occurred the night I pulled the covers over my head. My prayer for mercy was answered. It was answered in the blink of an eye, an eye that was trying to hide, seeking rest and a new perspective.

We were on a new path, but closely knit boundaries remained until school was out for the summer. Time was needed for each of us to build trust and confidence and to sort out the feelings behind the behavior. We had some wonderful moments together, and without doubt, we did our best work over giant scoops of Haggen Daz ice cream.

In lieu of traveling, I worked part-time in the office that spring. The program schedule was very full; they wanted help and were willing to accept what time I could give. The summer months were also looking to be quite busy and extra travel staff was badly needed. I was asked to work a program scheduled for June. Normally I did not work during the summer months because I wanted to be home when the kids were out of school. My heart leapt and said yes, I wanted to go, but my ego said no, I was needed at home. I wrestled with myself for a week before I accepted the assignment. As tempting as it can be to live in fear and doubt, I needed to move forward in trust and love. Sometimes that can be so very hard to do, but it begins with one small step.

When I stepped onto the plane to go to the mountains of North Carolina to help coordinate the events of a motorcycle rally, I had no idea what I had agreed to. I said goodbye to business suits, hotel ballrooms, famous motivational speakers, and black tie dinners and hello to barricading streets, dumpsters, porta-johns, and the beginning of a new spiritual path.

Our staff arrived several days early to prepare, although for what we weren't sure. We needed to reinvent the wheel. Nothing in our past work experiences had prepared us for the tasks at hand. We were in high gear and watching for signs that would lead us to the next step, which was a total mystery. This wasn't work. It was a wondrous adventure and incredible fun.

The day that the rally participants were to arrive in town and the rally was to officially begin, I was in the hotel parking lot checking on the tent that had been erected for one of the events. Not a soul was in sight. As I turned to walk back to the hotel lobby, I noticed two magnificently handsome, and significantly younger, men walking toward me. They were wearing typical motorcycle gear: boots, denim, and black leather. I didn't think a thing of their presence and changed course slightly so that we wouldn't meet head on. They changed course as well, and after brief introductions, we found ourselves in a serious discussion about life, particularly the vulnerability of teens. It was a very personal conversation to be having with people I'd just met, and amazingly, it spoke to the very reason I was standing on that spot at that very moment. The men and the conversation were fascinating.

Mitch and Larry spoke as if we were old friends, Mitch in particular. He was very affirming and made many references to situations that clearly mirrored what I had just experienced. He was radiant. He emanated a powerful energy that was beautifully soft and tender. I felt like I was being wrapped in the comfort of a loving hug, but we were standing three feet apart. I wondered what was going on. Who was this guy?

I was engaged in the conversation but also noticing that my heart was beating with a gentleness and warmth that I had never before experienced. I felt safe and loved. It seemed as though I had transcended space and time. Oops, I had. We had been talking for well over an hour. I needed to get back to work. As I dashed off they told me that they would see me later.

They were true to their word. I bumped into my two new friends often as I wrestled with barricades and traffic. I always felt their presence before I saw them. How odd! Each time, they had words of encouragement and support. I noticed that these affirmations more aptly applied to my real life and not to the tasks at hand. How curious!

After twelve long, hard, and fun-filled days, I was ready to go home. As the staff boarded the plane, a coworker told me that Mitch and Larry said they were going to bring extra helmets next year so they could take us riding. That sounded like fun, but who could know what a year would bring. More importantly, I had already decided that my tired, achy body didn't need to revisit this event. At that moment, if I had been asked to return as staff next year, I would have said no. It had been great fun, but enough was enough.

Returning home was uneventful. The laundry was piled high, and golden retriever hair was everywhere. I was thankful; life in our household was quite normal. I, however, was not. My heart was lighter, and the day-to-day challenges were much less bothersome. There was no explanation for the change, and I didn't need one. I was happier than I had ever been.

The summer days merrily rolled by. I tried to find a quiet space in each one. When I did, my motorcycle buddies invariably came to mind. I wondered if I would ever see them again, but it really didn't matter. I could feel the warmth of their presence. Somehow, they were with me.

As school began and life became busier, I thought of them less and less. There was little time for listening to the silence as more of the day was allocated to doing.

Spring returned, and I was asked to staff the motorcycle rally again, something that I had all but forgotten. Reluctantly I agreed to go. I was thinking more about the daunting weight of the barricades that I would be moving and less about the magic of my two special friends and the fun we had.

As I was checking into the hotel, I was reminded of the promised rides on the Blue Ridge Parkway, something that motorcyclists from all over the country come to do. It sounded like a wonderful adventure, but I didn't actually believe in the possibility of it happening. I wasn't even sure that it was something I really wanted to do.

Arrival day came. We were surrounded by thousands of motorcycles and enthusiastic riders. It was noisy and chaotic. I barely heard my walkie-talkie when a coworker asked my location. I was in a parking lot trying to sort out campers and trailers and motorcycles and wondering why I was in North Carolina when I could just as easily be sitting in my garden reading a good book. Within minutes my two special friends rode into the lot, complete with big smiles and extra helmets hooked to the back of their motorcycles. I was flabbergasted! They were just checking in and said they would find me later. I had no doubt that they would. And they did, often. Whenever I found five minutes to sit under a tree and take a break, they showed up. I was called to the scene of an accident; they had arrived before me and were the first to provide assistance. If I were in a restaurant eating, they would walk in.

One evening they joined four of us as we were grabbing a quick bite and a respite from the day. We were catching up on the past year. The conversation drifted to our jobs. Mitch began talking about the company where he worked. He described the company and the trucks they used in great detail. The others segued onto another topic while I listened attentively as he described the bright orange color of the eighteen-wheelers and the spelling of the company name, several times. I was unfamiliar with the company but there was little doubt that I would recognize one of the trucks if I happened upon one. It was a strange conversation, made stranger by my complete comfort with a man I knew virtually nothing about; a man who was tattooed, wearing a Grateful Dead tee-shirt, and sporting a belt buckle that was as big as my hand. It was embossed with a beautiful insignia and the words "Special Forces."

Oops! I had barricades to move. I excused myself. Again I was late. He had a way of making time stand still.

When I bumped into my pals the next day, they asked if I would like to go riding. I thanked them for the offer but told them I would be working until eleven p.m. That was not a problem. They offered to meet me at the hotel. I was shocked when I heard myself say that I would be there. Why was I agreeing to ride on the back of a motorcycle (something I would never have given the kids permission to do) late at night with two relative strangers in unfamiliar mountains? I had no answer. I just knew that I had never felt safer and more at peace than in the presence of these men. I felt I was supposed to go, and I did.

Every moment was glorious. The moon and stars were bright. The air was gentle and sweet with the delicate scent of lilacs in bloom. Occasionally the aroma of a wood-burning fire punctuated the moist air. The lights in the valleys below glowed softly and hinted at the many twists and turns of the mountainous terrain as we wound our way to nowhere. Perfection! My senses were totally alive, and I was completely at peace. I felt free as never before. I wasn't even holding on.

When they dropped me off, they promised more of the same the following night. I could hardly wait. When they picked me up, however, they said they had not eaten and somehow knew that I hadn't eaten as well. We went to a restaurant instead. We talked, and sang oldies, and filled ourselves with hot fudge sundaes buried in a mountain of luscious whipped cream.

Those two absolutely perfect evenings had nothing in common with one notable exception. Every time I expressed self-doubt or made a self-deprecating remark, I was told by Mitch, "You're okay." When I heard those words, my heart would resonate with a calming, warm energy that was wondrously soothing. There simply are not words to adequately describe how it felt.

We were all leaving the next day. When they dropped me off that night, they said they would see me next year, but somehow I knew differently. I would never see them again, and it seemed that was how it should be.

I arrived home exhausted but feeling exhilarated. As I walked into the house, the first question asked was, "Did you ride on a motorcycle?" The second was, "Why are you so happy?" I told the family about my adventures. I knew that we all had something to gain from my magical encounters. I went to bed feeling indescribable joy and hope. What would tomorrow bring?

Tomorrow brought eight loads of laundry, a house in need of

cleaning, and an empty refrigerator. Welcome back to the real world! I put off shopping as long as possible. I was still very tired and didn't relish the idea of driving anywhere. Finally, I knew I had no choice but to go.

About a mile from home I stopped for a red light. There, just crossing my path, was a very large, pumpkin orange, eighteen-wheeler fitting the exact description of the ones so carefully described to me a few nights earlier. As I was watching in disbelief, I heard, "You're okay," and felt a warm surge of energy in my heart. I was wrapped in a cloak of joy. My eyes welled with tears. The light changed and I had to move, but I didn't want to. I wanted to stay in that moment. I said, "Thank you," but I wasn't sure to whom and proceeded to the store.

While shopping, I wasn't able to stay focused on the grocery list; I had to go back within a couple of days to pick up the many forgotten items. As I was nearing the neighborhood shopping area, I sensed that I should go to the local bookstore, and I did. With no rhyme or reason, I walked straight to the table of books newly released in paperback. There sitting on the table was *God on a Harley*, by Joan Brady. My heart skipped several beats. How funny, I thought! Was this a joke? I picked it up and tentatively turned it over to read the back cover:

"Come out of the shadows, Christine. You've spent far too much time hiding in shadows." The man who spoke to her was gorgeous—long sable hair, faded T-shirt, black motorcycle jacket—all astride a 1340cc Harley-Davidson, mysteriously parked on a moonlit beach near her home. Christine was inexplicably drawn to this stranger—who seemed to know everything about her…"

I was dumbfounded, so much so that I asked a person near me to confirm the title of the book. It was *God on a Harley*. I hadn't lost all sense of reality, although I certainly entertained that thought. I didn't really know what to think, but I did laugh. Though I had not been working for Harley-Davidson, and my friends hadn't been riding Harleys, there was little question that I was buying the book.

As I walked out of the store, I looked up and was shocked to see an eighteen-wheeler driving by. It was a perfect match to the ones described by Mitch. This was getting interesting. Having never noticed them before, they suddenly were appearing with amazing regularity. On cue I heard "You're okay" and felt that familiar rush of warmth. Something, somewhere was trying to get my attention and had done precisely that. Again, I said, "Thank you!"

I was having such fun and wanted to share it, so when I got home, I put the book on the kitchen table and proceeded to unload the groceries. One by one, members of the family commented on the title. They tried to make jokes, but they clearly were not amused. They wanted life's mysteries to remain just that. I wanted more.

Once I began reading, I couldn't put the book down. It was a fictional story closely mirroring the very real experience I had just had; a chance meeting, an attraction that was indescribable, and proffered wisdom leading Christine to uncover her true spirit. Her "god" then moved on to help another, as I knew Mitch had moved on.

The events of the past few days were too synchronous to ignore. Clearly, coincidences aren't coincidences, and things happen when they are supposed to happen. I began to question the essence of Mitch's being. Who was he, really? At the moment I hadn't an answer, but I believed there was a reason I was led to the book.

Given the absence of answers, I was discovering the power of living with the questions. I felt free. Life suddenly had no bounds or limits. Anything really was possible.

They say, whoever "they" are, that we create our own reality. I wish I could say that I possessed the ingenuity to dream of meeting a beautiful spirit who would take me on a magical ride in the magnificent Blue Ridge Mountains and tell me at every turn that I was okay. I can't. Apparently we are given the help we need when we can't create it for ourselves or don't know where to look for it. It boggles my mind to consider that the extraordinary can occur on our behalf. Apparently, miracles aren't saved for special occasions or special people, and they don't necessarily arrive in spectacular ways. That we are so loved is a message I had often heard but never before truly believed.

Somewhere in the great beyond there was obviously some doubt that I would be accepting of this truth, because I was given a very large sign as a reminder. Every time I see one of those big old trucks I am reminded that I am loved and that I am okay, regardless of the situation I am experiencing. I see them often, most particularly when there has been a bump in my road. They feel so playful, and as I chuckle at their presence, I feel my heart radiate with warmth. I pause to give thanks.

The lesson was taken a step further when Susan's husband, Jim, called. He wanted to visit over the Fourth of July. Perfect! He wanted companionship and a few days at the lake, and I needed to talk to someone. We did talk about everything from kids and family to my motorcycle buddies. Besides my immediate family, there were only a few with whom I shared my adventure. I didn't want to invite the skepticism of others in before I had clarified my own feelings and thoughts. Jim was a trusted friend. I knew he would listen without judgment.

As we talked, I was trying to describe the presence of Mitch and unable to find words that did justice to the feelings. Jim interrupted.

"It was the light," he said. "You were attracted by the light." I had no idea what he was talking about. I was, however, reminded that I had neglected to ask him to bring along a book of his that I wanted to read. The book was about angels. I had given it to Jim the previous Christmas. He spoke of it often, and it sounded fascinating. I told him I was sorry that I had missed the opportunity to borrow it. He laughed. For some unknown reason, he had thrown it in the trunk of his car just before coming. The message was clear. I was to be learning about the angelic realm right now.

As never before, I felt that there truly was a plan and that I was a part of it. In that moment, I knew love—not the kind sold in the movies and romance novels but the love that is ever present and nonjudgmental. It just is.

Surrounded by the majesty of Lake Superior, I opened *Angelspeak*—and the next chapter in my life. The purpose of the book was to teach the reader how to communicate with angels. I will admit that I was hesitant, but what could I possibly lose by trying? With pencil and notebook in hand I began to ask questions of whomever might be listening and wrote down what I heard. I asked names. I asked how each was guiding me, and most importantly, I asked what they wanted me to know at that moment. I didn't have to ask about Mitch. By that time there was little question in my mind and heart that he was heaven sent. His purpose had been to guide me towards self-acceptance, and he was exactly what I needed—exactly when I needed it.

I called on the angels regularly. When communicating with them, I didn't always hear what I wanted to hear. To trust or not to trust—how was I to discern between the voice of my ego and the voice of the spiritual realm? The response to that question often came in Mitch's words, "Life is a journey, not a guided tour." That may be true, but it didn't help. My pragmatic nature was looking for the answers to be spelled out in blazing neon lights.

When I would find myself particularly unsure and confused, I would typically feel a desire to go to the bookstore. I normally preferred to frequent small, independent stores, but I had a strong sense that I was to go to the local outlet of a national chain. Not too surprisingly, when I honored the feeling and went to that bookstore, I would find a book that answered my most immediate question within steps of the entrance. I have purchased a plethora of books, each lovingly selected by the angelic host that was busy trying to save me from myself. I will admit to sometimes ignoring the guidance given. So often I was too focused on day-to-day living to see the spirit of life that surrounds us. How grateful I am for the many opportunities presented to me so that I might learn to see.

What gifts I had been given! My perceptions of life were changing, and I was seeing with new eyes. I had been lovingly guided into a very real awareness of the spirit world and our connection to it. When I was stuck or not believing, I was led to the wisdom and experiences of others through books. When life seemed bleak, I would see one of those silly old trucks and know that whatever was happening, I was okay. I was beginning to understand the true power of God. It really was limitless and unconditional and ever present. I was breathing it in and feeling it. I was loved, and I didn't have to do a thing to deserve it. It just is that way for us all. Regardless of how many times I stumbled or resisted, I was loved just because. The possibilities truly are without bounds and are far greater than anything I could ever have imagined. All we have to be is willing. The rest is being provided.

The Most Powerful
Gifts Are Those
We Give Ourselves

We each have our own motivation for change. Mine was to be happier and to free myself from the confines of the roles I had created. Whenever possible, for the remainder of the summer, I sat on my favorite bench in the garden or in a warm, soothing tub and read. It became the norm, no longer a luxury. The laundry could wait. I was being guided to books about spirit and self-discovery. I had previously been averse to *how to's*, but this became a purposeful quest. Each book became a friend affirming that there is purpose in life's journey and helping me to define my own. Sometimes they even suggested the next step. Reading about others' experiences helped me to better understand my own. I soaked up the wisdom of the Dalai Lama, Deepak Chopra, Carolyn Myss, Brian Weiss, and many others. I journaled and mused and would often pose my newest question at the dinner table. Life was exhilarating.

I was particularly fascinated by what others believed love to be. What is love, really? Marianne Williamson, in her book *Return to Love,* says that it is participatory. I interpret that to mean that love requires action. It seemed simple, but for me it wasn't. I was doing a great deal for others, but it didn't always bring a warm, fuzzy glow to the recipient or to me. There was more to it; motivation and expectation probably had something to do with the outcome.

I had found a new path that held the promise of some interesting new adventures and questions. My ability to find answers was, and still is, directly related to my willingness to change. It is often so much easier to stay put, in the familiar, resisting change. Anthony De Mello makes an interesting point in his book *Awareness*. He suggests that it isn't the unknown that we fear. It is the loss of the known. I think that is a very subtle but important difference. We try to hold onto the familiar for dear life, and that is exactly what we are sacrificing by holding on, our dear lives. We aren't conditioned to look for the door that is opening as another closes. We often choose to be blind to opportunity until the pain is so great that we must do something different; we can no longer stay where we are. I had been there, and I never wanted to go back.

Yogananda, a Hindu yogi, suggests that when we are willing to go to any lengths to find enlightenment, the teacher is always nearby. I was learning to be open to the teachers presented: a kind act, words to a song, a wagging tail, a gentle breeze, or sage advice. Essentially, everything in our midst can teach us something.

I attended a workshop on centering prayer, with great reluctance I might add. The subject was something I knew nothing about and wasn't sure that I wanted to explore. But, every time I tried to throw the flier away, I had a nagging feeling that I should reconsider. I signed up two days before the event and am grateful that I did. It was a magical day.

I was pleasantly surprised to find that centering prayer is simply a form of meditation taught with a Christian perspective. It invites us to take time out of each precious day to go within, to be still, and to find peace in the stillness. On the one hand, it is a very difficult thing to do in our busy culture, and on the other hand, it is a means of surviving our busy culture. Quieting the mind and going within, so simple and so powerful!

I had been meditating, but prior to the workshop I hadn't known to call it that. Whenever I really needed to hear the voice within, I knew to head for the garden or the bathtub and listen to the silence, but I had never entertained the thought of developing a regular practice. Before me was an answer—being delivered by an enchanting instructor who was both joyful and inspired. Patricia's wisdom was laced with a thick Peruvian accent that added to the pleasure of the day.

Just prior to closing the workshop, Patricia announced that she was teaching a Tai Ji class beginning the following week, again, Tai Ji was something I knew nothing about. My daughter had been looking for a Tai Ji instructor, so I took the information home. A few days later, I found myself driving her to class at the Benedictine Monastery. Knowing that I would be waiting while my daughter was in class, I brought with me the most recent find from the bookstore. I thought the peace and quiet of the monastery would be the ideal place to savor the latest addition to my library. I never got the chance. No sooner had I settled into a comfy chair than I heard, "Take off your shoes and come to class!"

"Me? I am just waiting for my daughter, thank you."

"Do you know what Tai Ji is?"

"No."

"You will never find out if you don't come to class."

Obediently I took off my shoes and joined the circle. The next ninety minutes were delightful. We were taught slow, purposeful movements to sacred music that honored our bodies and the God within. I felt connected and freed all at the same time. I was hooked and ended up studying with Patricia for two years; my daughter moved on to other interests shortly after we began. She had served her purpose by getting me there. So often we are present for the sake of another.

One of the many benefits of Tai Ji was gaining more flexibility in my lower back. After several years, it was still causing occasional discomfort. Another benefit was that I was meeting people who embraced the world of metaphysics. They spoke of a chakra system. I was curious, so I began to read about it. I discovered that the chakra system is comprised of centers of energy in the body. Though invisible to the eye, many cultures have believed in its existence for thousands of years. The balance, or imbalance, of each energy center is believed to be related to our physical, spiritual, and emotional health. I was intrigued.

The first chakra, or root, includes the spine. When the root chakra is out of balance, feelings of low self-esteem, of not belonging, or of not trusting that needs will be met may exist. Acknowledging choice, nurturing oneself, and believing in oneself are ways to regain balance. The dis-ease in my life accurately matched the description of an imbalance in the first chakra. I was looking at another answer and proof enough for me that there is a profound connection between how we feel about ourselves and our physical well being. Can we truly heal by addressing the needs of the physical body alone? It didn't seem so. The spirit and emotional bodies apparently need to be tended to as well.

Tai Ji combined all three. It was freeing the stiffness in my body and my heart through the intertwining of a Christian perspective, physical movement, and sacred music. I was learning to accept myself just as I was, two left feet and all.

At about the same time, a casual acquaintance I hadn't seen for months and haven't seen since, told me about a qigong master teaching at a local community college. She knew only that qigong was a form of Chinese energy healing that has been practiced for thousands of years. She had experienced significant relief from her debilitating arthritis following her first class with Master Lin, and she suggested that I go. I called for information. The timing was impeccable; the next level one class was to begin in two weeks. It seemed like a very long time to wait.

For me, Spring Forest Qigong created the opportunity for physical healing through the strengthening of spiritual energy. Inviting Universal Energy into our lives to remove blockages in our energy system and relieve the pain and dis-ease is an unquestionable journey of faith. There is no physical manipulation or touching in qigong. Qigong is a belief system. It is through the presence of God that we find balance and healing. Qigong teaches that we are one, and that we are connected to the Source and all that surrounds us. It reflects the shared truths of the great masters and religions such as Christianity, Buddhism and Tao. We are all one. This is the simplest of messages, and I believe it to be the most profound.

Spring Forest Qigong is message-healing, meaning that the messages we give ourselves create our reality. A door opened, and I was presented with the opportunity to revisit the messages I was giving myself and to discover what I believed about my life. We can choose to be accepting of ourselves and celebrate our very being or be judgmental and put ourselves down. What we decide about ourselves is what becomes real, and it affects everything in our lives including our health.

We heal when we invite love, or God, or Universal Energy—it matters not what you name it—into our lives. Be it spiritual, emotional, physical healing, or a combination thereof, it comes if we open the door, often in unexpected ways. It is not for us to decide what should happen or how we are to heal. We are given what we need—when we need it. It is a path paved by faith. We can only see the gifts given when we abandon the need to control, free ourselves of expectations and *must have's*, and be accepting of what enters our lives. Everything that comes into our lives is an opportunity if we wish to view it as such. When we invite the Creator to live in us and through us, we are doing just that.

*Change
Is a Gift
for All*

understand that change can be difficult for us all and is not welcomed by many, regardless of who is making the changes. I had found many things that I wanted to change in myself—patterns of communicating, how I allocated my time, and beliefs about myself. Some significant adults in my life were very resistant to the changes I was making, and I sensed a very clear opposition to my growth. The presence of angels was questioned, and energy healing seemed doubtful. Meditation was thought to be unproductive, and others sometimes felt rejection if I chose to be in silence rather than to participate in an activity. The "tribal leaders" wanted to keep me in a place that felt safe to them. They often reminded me where that place should be, to be like them, and to do what they were doing. My charging into the unfamiliar was not a part of their plan for me or for themselves. They, too, proved to be magnificent teachers.

Although it was sometimes frustrating to me that they did not readily accept who I was becoming, their lack of acceptance served a great purpose—the same purpose that it had been serving my entire life. When I faced resistance, I had a choice. I could be defensive and become angry, or I could take the opportunity to look at the differences between us and separate their truths from mine. My way wasn't the only way, but I believed it to be a viable way. From my new perspective, there didn't have to be rights and wrongs, just understanding of the differences.

As I made changes, it undoubtedly presented challenges for others. They, too, had the option of reevaluating the beliefs they held and the directions of their lives, but I didn't expect that others would change. What I really wanted was for us to help each other be the very best we could be. For me, that included honoring our different paths. *Love* is a verb. So is *to accept*. So is sharing who we truly are at any moment in time. So also is *change*, and allowing for change may be the most loving thing we can do for ourselves and for others.

Through a fellow Tai Ji student, I learned of a convent that offered a nine-day silent retreat. If I so chose, Patricia, our instructor, would be my spiritual director on the retreat, whatever a spiritual director was. There was a lot of teasing about my ability to be silent for nine seconds let alone nine days. I laughed as I sent in my registration.

Any questions I may have had about attending the retreat were quieted the day before I was to go. I felt a need to go to the bookstore and found Joan Anderson's *A Year by the Sea*, a book about the author's sabbatical from her thirty-year marriage. As I picked it off the shelf, I felt a warm, soft energy move through my body. Without even opening the cover, I felt the comfort of an old friend. I took it home and packed it to take on the retreat.

Arriving at Villa Maria, I discovered that I would be sharing my silent space with thirty-two nuns, two priests, three spiritual directors, a reiki master, a massage therapist, and a young woman who wanted a quiet place to needlepoint Christmas gifts. Not even Catholic, I was definitely in unfamiliar waters. As we gathered for dinner that first evening, we were allowed to speak with each other. It was a lovely group, and they warmly welcomed this novice into their world. I still had no idea what was ahead of me, but I didn't care. It just felt so wonderful to be there!

Following the meal, I went to my room to begin reading *A Year by the Sea*. As I read, I felt like I was looking into a mirror. This captivating story is about a woman who was searching for the essence of her being. Wanting to connect with life and unsure how to do so, she moved, by herself, to the comfort of the family cottage. She had no plans but simply allowed each day to unfold, meeting her needs as they arose. She had a year. I had only eight days left to sort and sift. It was what I was able to give myself for the moment, and I knew it would be enough.

I read late into the night finishing the book. I had been unable to put it down, so closely did it match my feelings and experiences of late. The author, too, had few answers but was discovering the questions. It was reassuring to know of someone who was in a situation similar to mine and willing to be honest about it.

Morning came all too quickly. The day began outside at sunrise with Tai Ji. It was a beautiful way to connect with the spirit in nature and set a peaceful tone for the day. Following breakfast I met with Patricia for my first encounter with spiritual direction. The first order of the day was to identify my focus for the retreat. I had not come with an agenda; it never occurred to me that I should. That was frustrating to Patricia as everyone else had. My belief that things always work out was not much comfort to her.

Finally she said, "You don't speak of your husband. Tell me about your relationship." I simply explained that it was what it was. We were not particularly close, and I believed I ranked in importance somewhere below his work and his passion for golf. Making changes in the relationship didn't seem to be an option, and I was accepting of that. Her eyes brightened and she asked, "How is your life like a golf course?" She offered a few verses from the Gospel of Matthew to bring clarity as I searched for an answer to her question, and she sent me on my way.

Patricia had posed an interesting question, but she had been uncharacteristically sharp and impatient. For sure I was going to find an answer before I met with her the next morning.

Because it was a beautiful spring day, I decided to find my answers in the out-of-doors. I took a bike ride, hiked, walked the labyrinth, and sat under a tree with my journal and a copy of the New Testament close at hand. Images of golf courses flowed into the space left vacant by the absence of intentional thought. I saw in them places to escape from everyday responsibilities and connect with friends. A golf course can be an extension of the office or a place to compete with others or oneself.

Golf courses are manmade and seem to be very high maintenance. They are normally well manicured; the watering and mowing appear to be never-ending. The gardens surrounding the clubhouse are typically organized in formal rows and designs, sometimes even replicating a logo and most often containing annual bedding plants.

There are many forms of control on a golf course: fertilizer to encourage growth, herbicides to eradicate undesirables, and pesticides to kill things that munch on roots, leaves, and ankles. Some courses are public. Others are private with restrictions that govern who can and cannot play. There are usually expectations surrounding what you wear when you play golf and the pace you must maintain. The game itself has many rules and regulations.

Questions surfaced in my mind. Was I relying on artificial stimulation to maintain and preserve my balance, or was I finding it naturally? How did I play? Was I competing, and with whom? Was there room for spontaneity in my life, or was I most comfortable with order and rules to guide? Was I using "members only" signs as a means of control and protection and, if so, from what? How does my garden grow?

The answers came rather quickly in a vision of my own back yard. The long, sturdy arms of an old oak tree bathe the yard in deep, cool shade; the light is dappled and soft. My favorite place of rest is on a teak bench that sits upon a patio made of old paving bricks. They have been scavenged from many places. Though similar in size, each brick has its own unique character—a chink that is missing, a corner that has broken away, or a name that was embossed on it eons ago by the manufacturer. In combination they beckon with their simple beauty.

The patio is bordered by perennial gardens, as is the picket fence that encircles the yard. Shade plants predominate, and I rely on texture to create appeal. There is little variety in my garden as so few species thrive in the limited sunlight. Sprinkled among the varying tints of green are muted pinks and blues with bits of white to reflect the moonlight. There are no rows and little obvious order. I often let volunteer seedlings be. Maybe they know more than I.

I fertilize lightly in the spring, preferring to offer grass clippings, mulched leaves, peat, and other natural sources of nutrition and texture to the soil. The grass is a touch long—providing a natural barrier to weeds. I don't use chemicals that could harm the dog or the other critters that frolic in the yard. I love the bunnies and squirrels that gather. All are welcome.

The bushes in my yard are a bit wild. I like the branches that take an unexpected turn as they reach for the sky. How would life be if I lived each day with my arms opened wide and with my face turned towards the sun?

I realized that was precisely the direction I wanted my life to take. I didn't want to be shaped by others or look exactly like my neighbor. I wanted to grow at my own pace and in the space and manner of my own choosing. My garden is a reflection of that. I feel at peace when we are together.

Patricia's question was as magical as the day. Just before falling asleep that night, I counted my blessings and added silence to the list. It is a beautiful companion. It speaks the truth.

Morning came again and with it the peace of Tai Ji and the tenacity of Patricia. She didn't want to know what I had learned about the golf course. I had learned what I needed to, and that was enough. I had read the entire book of Matthew instead of the few suggested verses, and I had some questions.

That led to a discussion of attachments; Patricia wanted to know about mine. She wasn't referring to material possessions but was asking about the belief systems that I was using to define, and possibly limit, myself. She apologized for being brusque the previous day and said that she had no idea where her questions were coming from. I was not surprised. I trusted that the work I was to be doing on the retreat would be presented, one way or another, and it was. Everything was as it should be, including Patricia's uncharacteristic demeanor. It served to get my attention, and my focus was narrowed to what was immediately before me and to the opportunity being presented. Patricia suggested a few verses in Mark, and I was on my way to another perfect day.

The weather was glorious so, again, I was outside walking the labyrinth and hiking. I found a furnished cabin with a fireplace and a screened-in porch on the Villa property. "Just because," I had thrown a sleeping bag in the car before coming. Now I knew why. I asked the director for permission to use the cabin and for a book of matches. I was given both. And while I was in her office, I signed up for a massage and a reike treatment. I might as well do it all.

As the sun set, I lit a fire in the fireplace of my new home away from home. I spent hours watching the flames. I thought about my definition of *family* and the part I wanted to play in mine versus the part I thought I should play. I questioned the line between my responsibility to the whole and to myself. Thoughts about the difference between selfishness and taking care of oneself swirled around me like smoke from the fire. From my bed on the porch, I watched the moon rise and the stars twinkle. Listening to the sounds of the nearby critters, and they were very nearby, I drifted into another peaceful sleep.

The days passed with a gentle rhythm with Tai Ji at sunrise and more Tai Ji privately with Patricia after breakfast. We decided that complete silence was what I needed. If more questions were to come, I had faith they would find me. I read the last two Gospels and spent most of each day outside. I ended each perfect day with a fire and a complete sense of calm. I was in heaven.

The questions flowed into my consciousness in their own time. The perfect vehicle for clarifying was always nearby, be it scripture, the labyrinth, the shape of a flame, or the voice within. The ebb and flow was gentle and ever present.

One day I was looking for something a little different to do when I found jigsaw puzzles in the dining room. I chose to work a 500-piece picture of tiny jelly beans; it just isn't my style to do anything that looks easy. I sorted the straight outside edges and corners from the inside pieces and put the frame together. The connection of one piece to another firmed and strengthened the foundation of the puzzle. As I searched for the exact color and shape needed to fill an empty space, I noticed the similarities in the pieces and the subtlety of the differences. Each was individual in its own right, and each was needed for completion of the whole—with no one piece being more valuable than another.

The puzzle was a beautiful metaphor for life. I had been looking for a particular piece off and on the entire time I was putting the puzzle together only to find in the end that it was missing.

I was learning to see teachers in all that was around me, and in the stillness of the Villa and its environs, they were very apparent. I did not want to leave, but it was time to go home and incorporate stillness and peace into my everyday life. I quickly settled back into the normal routine at home but with a different perspective. Life was gentle. There was less focus on being busy and more on listening to the silence. I knew joy, not the fun of being with a friend or laughing at a joke, but that feeling of happiness within regardless of the circumstances of the moment. There is a saying, "Serenity is not freedom from the storm but peace within the storm." I finally knew what that really meant.

Having a new perspective opened doors for new opportunities, glorious ones. I heard of a woman who served as a channel for a spirit guide. I was curious and wanted to make an appointment. I got what I thought to be her name and number and called. We talked for ten minutes; nothing was making sense. I finally asked to whom I was speaking. She was a psychic with a private practice and classes in psychic development beginning in a couple of weeks, not the woman who channeled. Had I been given the wrong number? I didn't really think so. I made an appointment for a psychic reading and signed up for the classes.

Kathy was amazing. I went to the reading with a list of questions per her request and didn't have to ask one. Her reading touched them all. She placed the things that were happening around and within me in a framework of purpose. It was becoming very clear that there simply are no accidents. I knew that, but I didn't always want to believe it. She helped me to see that there was a path connecting what looked to be random events.

Kathy's classes were fascinating as well. She was quite gifted at leading guided meditations. Each week we would find ourselves in beautiful imagery that led us to our very being and helped us to discover what was overshadowing the song in our hearts. She created a very safe environment and made it easy to explore questions of limiting behaviors. How had we let others and their belief systems define us? What did we believe about ourselves, and did those beliefs inhibit our spirits or release them? These were not new questions, but offered in a different light, they created new insight.

We talked of walls and boundaries. Walls were defined as beliefs that have been taught to us by others, typically our families. They are given to us as guides, often lovingly, and we accept them as truths, but they aren't based on our own experiences. They are delivered within the confines of what others believe we should or shouldn't believe and do. Walls put life in the framework of *do* and *don't, right* and *wrong, good* and *bad*. They are handed down in the form of judgments and are rigid. When we accept the limitations that walls place in our lives, our responses and actions are then based on the expectations of others. Walls exist because change is feared.

Boundaries on the other hand are constantly moving. They represent choice, the choices we make. With boundaries we create a space for ourselves that changes as we grow. While boundary lines are fluid because they change as we change, they also have definition. They are defined by our experiences and by what we wish to allow into our lives. What do we choose to say yes to, and when do we say no? It is a matter of choice, our choice.

We all have walls and boundaries in our lives. I believe part of our job is to discern which is which and rid our lives of the walls. Am I listening to the voice of others or to my own?

Understanding the difference between walls and boundaries helped me discover a pattern of behavior that was very limiting. It began in childhood and was so very much a part of me that it was difficult to distinguish between the pattern and me. If what I believed to be true wasn't reflected by those around me, I assumed that I was wrong. How it began I do not know. I don't know that it matters. What is important is that somewhere along the line, I accepted that my feelings and beliefs were wrong when they were not in agreement with those of others. I seemed to be wrong much of the time. That rarely stopped me from acting in alignment with my belief system, but on occasion it did create conflict. I didn't fit the mold and judgment resulted, sometimes by others and sometimes by myself.

My view of the world seemed to be different from others. I didn't really care about the latest styles or what parties I was invited to. I preferred to forge my own way. For example, I could never explain why I chose to adopt three of our four children. I didn't feel I needed to explain it. I just felt that it was the way I was to go. "Why not?" was the only response that made sense to me when questioned. I didn't see risk. I saw opportunity, the same miraculous opportunity presented by live birth.

More than once I wondered if there really was something wrong with me. Maybe I was hurting others and myself and was just not able to see it, as was sometimes suggested. By doing things "my way," was I truly attempting to control others, as was also suggested, or was I simply honoring my own path? I struggled to find the balance between self-confidence and self-doubt. I worked to find compromise. I sometimes gave in, but I never give up.

I didn't understand why there was seemingly so much opposition to what I believed to be the essence of me. My feelings didn't seem to matter, and my opinions were regularly dismissed. I called myself the invisible woman, and in reality I was, but it was to myself that I was invisible. Others were treating me as if I were invisible because they were reflecting how I treated myself. I heard that I was wrong when I believed that I might be. My feelings were ignored by others when I wasn't honoring them myself.

Seeds of doubt were sewn—seeds that I allowed to grow, seeds that I watered every time I put myself down, seeds that sprouted every time the opinion of another was held in higher regard than my own sense of knowing. They were seeds born in the climate of rights and wrongs and fertilized by the belief that we should all be reaching for the same star. The seeds thrived because I didn't believe that I held the answers for myself. The conflict was mine— being mirrored by those close to me.

I didn't have to agree with others to find acceptance. I needed to accept myself, just as I am. I didn't have to be like others to fit in. I had to trust in the essence of my being and discover that we are one. And I didn't need the love of another to feel complete and experience joy. I needed only the awareness of the God within.

I began to see that there was great purpose in the questions and the doubts and in the relationships that had been contentious and uncomfortable. They were teachers; they were beautiful gifts. They helped me to uncover the beliefs that I held toward myself that limited my ability to soar.

The missing piece of the puzzle had been found. I call it personal responsibility. I, and I alone, am responsible for all that I experience. If I believe there is a reason, a purpose for all that comes into my life, and if I accept that all experiences have value, then I can choose the response. I can learn from each situation, or I can deny that there is goodness in all things. I can grow and be grateful for the opportunity, or I can be angry, frustrated, and a victim. I can see differences and be accepting, or I can judge. My response depends on whether or not I see opportunity in the situation before me, and if I am aware that I have choice.

We all have the same right to make choices. How gentle life is when we suspend judgment of others and ourselves and accept that we are where we are for a reason, one that may be unknown to us at the moment, but purposeful nevertheless. I believe we all want to be loved for who we are at our very essence and not be told what we should or could be if only....

Believing that we are ultimately responsible for ourselves eliminates blame. No one can impact us if we don't choose to be impacted. Regardless of the situation, I get to select my response. No one else really has the power to make me angry or sad or joyful.

I can react that way, but I don't have to. It is up to me. I can be exactly who I want to be in any given moment, and knowing that I am the one with the power over my feelings and responses makes all the difference.

Taking personal responsibility also eliminates the need for guilt. We cannot impact someone else unless they choose it. I may be the cause of a situation, but I have no control over another's response. They also have the power of choice. If they are angry, it is of their own choosing. There is always the option to be understanding, compassionate, or serene in the eye of the storm. I will take responsibility for my actions, but I am not responsible for how someone else is feeling.

Life is so much richer when we are in control, not of what goes on around us, but of how we deal with situations as they arise. We don't have to be influenced by what others do or say; we get to choose how we respond. The issue is not what someone has done to us but what we have done to ourselves. The last line of Barbara Kingsolver's book *Prodigal Summer* is, "Every choice is a world made new for the chosen." I believe that we are all chosen. Exactly what world are we choosing to create for ourselves? Serenity is possible in the eye of the storm. It just takes practice.

The issue of personal responsibility had been surfacing for a long time. At first glance, it seemed irresponsible to absolve myself of guilt and blame. I was the mom. When someone or something was out of kilter I often questioned whether I had done enough or said too much or said too little. I had unwittingly assumed responsibility for much of what others did or felt. Not only was I carrying burdens that didn't belong to me, I was making it unnecessary for others to take responsibility for themselves. I had inadvertently tipped the scales and needed to regain the balance.

Changing my negative patterns of interaction was challenging, particularly when others didn't see a need to change as well. Nevertheless, I wanted to stay in relationship with the people that I love and be at peace with them and with our combined purpose.

I asked many people how to do just that and read many books before I discovered a very wise shaman who suggested that what we all really want is to be heard. We want validation that we are worthy regardless of the circumstances. She suggested that the next time I found myself in a situation where someone was upset, I simply ask, "What do you need?"

I did just that when a situation presented itself. The response caught me off guard. I was given a list of about ten things that the other person thought I needed to change. The tables had been turned. I stayed focused by taking a deep breath and asked again. Because I had not taken a defensive posture or gone on the attack, the other person seriously entertained my question. It only took a moment or two of thoughtfulness to discover what was really needed. There was fear surrounding a change in living arrangements, and what was needed was understanding that the fear existed and reassurance that everything would work itself out. How much more gratifying it was to embrace each other with a hug than to glare at each other in the heat of battle. It only took acceptance of what was—the fear that was present—and living in the moment, rather than digging up the past or forging into the future, to find peace.

When I am feeling out of sorts, I try to remember to ask myself what I am afraid of. Always, a doubt or frustration has crept in, and I have ventured into the past or am trying to determine the future. What I am needing is to return to my center, the present, the now. By asking the question, I am able to do just that.

"Some say that there are no mistakes, just lessons to be learned," are the words of a favorite song of mine. I believe that, and the people I know and love must be delighted that I am finally figuring it out. Each choice we make can teach regardless of the outcome. If the outcome doesn't suit us, we can then make a different choice.

When we open a door by choice, we open to the possibility of change and create an opportunity for others to walk through with us. It is surprising to me how often they do.

We Must Be Willing
to Receive
What Is Offered

One thing always leads to another. A fellow student of Kathy's recommended another psychic development teacher who used different methods to expand awareness of what lies beyond the five senses. I called to see about classes, and sure enough, Shari was beginning a new series in a couple of weeks. I have noticed that whenever I wish to entertain a new perspective, the opportunity to do so presents itself almost immediately. Universal timing is magical. I signed up for the course.

The first night, Shari explained that she was going to show us a variety of ways to expand our psychic awareness. Our homework for the week was to go shopping with the angels. She asked us to find a quiet time and ask our angels who we were to buy for, what we were to purchase, and where. Then we were to actually make the purchase.

A few days before class, I asked my angels for guidance. "Who am I to shop for?" I was given the name of one of my daughters. "What am I supposed to buy for her?" A vase, was the reply. That seemed strange to me. I had given that daughter a hand-blown vase for Christmas. Trying not to let my ego get involved, I asked where I was to make this purchase and was directed to go to Target.

I added a fourth question of my own. "Why am I buying the same gift, for the same person, from the same store?"

"Because someone is giving her a bucket load of flowers," was the response. With that, I had a vision of a tall, thin, galvanized bucket. This shopping trip was beginning to look like fun.

That evening I asked my husband if he would like to go to Target with me. I explained why, and he was intrigued. We searched high and low in what I thought were the obvious places for this gift. We found nothing. My husband suggested that we look in the garden department. I was thankful for his suggestion. I had run out of ideas and hadn't thought to ask the angels for help.

He took one aisle and I took another. I was beginning to question the whole adventure when I heard, "Judy, is this what you are looking for?" He had found a display of "French Buckets." They matched the picture in my mind's eye, and it seemed all the more perfect that he had been led to them. It was a very special gift for our daughter and a delightful lesson in listening for me. And, yes, she had just started to date a man who loved to bring her flowers. The angels knew.

Over the next three months, Shari led the class through a variety of exercises that showed us how to connect with the spirit world. She saved the best, energy healing, for last. For me that is the ultimate connection. It felt like going home. I wanted more.

I signed up for Master Lin's level two qigong class and also attended workshops led by a Catholic priest from India who had studied years earlier with a healer in the Philippines. He loved to joke about doing missionary work in the United States, and, truthfully, he was. The spirit was so alive in this man! Being in his presence was a gift in itself, and that, too, can be said of Master Lin. Their faith in the Universe, or God, whichever you choose to call it, is absolute. They are joyful and trusting. You can feel the peaceful energy that surrounds them. They have crossed the boundaries of religion, race, and nationality and believe in oneness. We are all one. It is really that simple, and life is so simple when you embrace this belief.

There are many techniques and names for healing with energy, and I have studied several. They all boil down to a very basic truth. When you open yourself to the power of the Creator, you will receive exactly what you need —exactly when you need it. That, however, may not be the same as what you want—when you want it.

Through the aid of many magnificent teachers, I was connecting with my spirit and deepening my faith. I was also learning to untangle my emotions and find balance on this plane. I didn't consciously select a direction to move in. The doors opened of their own accord, and I saw the opportunity or I didn't, depending on my attitude and the length of the to-do list. When an opportunity was missed, it would eventually return. Quite possibly appearing in a different form, but appearing nonetheless. The Universe is truly compassionate and forgiving. There are no mistakes, but sometimes there is confusion or a lapse in focus or an ego that just refuses to take a back seat. Always, I am thankful for a second chance and the sense of humor that allows me to see it.

I hadn't heard from the bookstore angel in awhile. I will never know if I hadn't been listening or if he had been on vacation. Driving toward the grocery store one day I received a message to go to the bookstore, and I did. I looked in two of my favorite places, New in Paperback and New Non-fiction. Finding nothing, I started for the New Age shelves in the back of the store when I "heard" a message to go to the Best Seller section. My ego was determined to guide the search, and I ignored the message. Finding nothing in New Age, I started toward the door. Luckily, I had to walk right by Best Sellers. I remembered the message to look there as I spotted a small book with flowers on the cover. I picked it up; it felt like it belonged in my hands. I walked to the checkout line without even looking at the title. I said, "Thank you," because I was grateful for the second chance.

The book I was holding was *The Four Agreements: A Toltec Wisdom Book*, by Miguel Ruiz. I didn't know what a Toltec was, and I was intrigued.

The Toltec community is an ancient collective of scientific leaders and artisans who lived in Mexico. Their spiritual beliefs and teachings have been passed down from generation to generation.

Don Miguel is a descendant and is passing on the age-old wisdom:

1. Be impeccable with your word.
2. Don't take anything personally.
3. Make no assumptions.
4. Always do your best.

As he illuminates the agreements, Don Miguel introduces the idea of domestication. He believes we come into this world and are trained to think a certain way, to do things a certain way, and to be like the others in our midst. There is no harm intended; our elders are motivated by love. They are simply passing on what they know. It is that way for everyone. We do it to our own children as well. I know that I surely did. As we develop our awareness, it is our job to peel away what we have been taught and find our own truths.

This was a new spin on the struggles I had been experiencing—the push of the individual away from the roots and the pull of the group to keep things as they are. It was a natural cycle but also a tug of war. With a new insight, my perspective on family relationships changed. I understood that the pattern had purpose and with understanding came compassion. Everyone had always been doing his best, including me.

Toltec wisdom is profound, and like everything else that has guided me on this path, so simple. The book was a blessing—the perfect message at the perfect time. I have shared it with many.

I am often amazed at the variety of people and experiences that have presented themselves as teachers. Each of the classes I have taken, the books I have read, and the people I have met have offered a special gift, an insight or an answer to a question. We need nothing on this journey but to be open and willing to explore life's offerings. Each road taken has offered new wisdom and understanding. But each has brought me back to the same place, seeing and feeling the ever-presence of God and the abundance of love for us all.

The Gift
of Letting Go

So, why did I ask for a divorce after thirty-two years of marriage? That question was asked of me often. There were many answers. Some were born in frustration and some arose from pain. But the one coming from truth was that I had changed. It was just that simple. I had learned to see with eyes of wonder. Invitations to join me on this amazing adventure were not accepted by my husband or, quite possibly, not understood. There had been moments of connection, like the angel shopping trip, but they were so very rare. They would give me hope and keep me invested for another several months, but they were too infrequent to build a sense of intimacy. He didn't want what I was working toward. I didn't want a relationship based on sharing four walls and a joint checking account. I was looking for a relationship centered on willingness—that being the willingness to approach each day with an open heart and find beauty in whatever was unfolding before us.

When he was able to articulate what he wanted for this lifetime, which was so very different than what I was choosing, I just let go. He drifted farther and farther away. The kids were essentially grown and independent of our daily routines, so there were no excuses for maintaining the status quo other than the desire to do so; I had none. We each had our individual paths, and we both deserved to live the way of our own choosing. There were no rights or wrongs, only differences in what we believed living to be. The relationship had run its course. I no longer found purpose in our being together.

There had been purpose in the beginning. When we married, we had many things in common. Both our lives had been colored by the expectations of others. Neither of us had explored our own uniqueness. As we reached for independence from our families and searched to find our own place in this world, we provided support for each other. The decisions we made were safe and practical. We were intent on building a stable foundation for the family we also wanted to build, and we did so within the confines of the structures that had been built for us.

Spiritually we were similar as well. I had little sense of my true essence, and he lacked understanding of his own. We were a good match, serving as mirrors for each other. It is no wonder that I felt so very comfortable in his presence. He treated me the same way I was treating myself. I was happy, or I thought I was. We had landed a part of the American dream, and we were reaching for the rest.

I don't remember feeling much anger or frustration prior to being married. After taking on my new roles as wife and caretaker, I began to lose sight of my own identity, and I didn't see it happening. When I began ignoring my needs in favor of others and treating myself as the invisible woman, my reflection—my husband—typically saw me the same way. It was two against none, and I didn't like it. Deep down, I knew that there must surely be another way. That is what gave birth to my frustration. My spirit knew that I was lovable, but I wasn't acting accordingly. I was at war with myself. No one else was needed for me to be in conflict, but the person that I believed to be my life partner was reflecting back my worst fears. Each shared experience was an opportunity to remember who I was at the core or to ignore it and get caught in a cycle of judgment and anger.

I knew something was amiss in my life, but I had no idea what it was or where I would find it. I wanted an answer though, so I began to say yes to the new opportunities that life presented. They came in every size and shape imaginable, usually right to the front door. I rarely had to go looking. I tried to make choices based on intuitive feelings, not on history or the expectations of others. When I did, I found joy. I discovered that the perceived risks surrounding my choices presented no real danger and typically opened doors to new and exciting worlds. Many of the walls that had been built by others to keep me safe began to crumble.

I managed the home front while my husband managed a career. Our lives were actually quite separate, but together we created a complete package. There was purpose in our being together.

Susan's death caused the direction of my life to change dramatically. Life became more precious to me. I no longer felt that it could be taken for granted or placed on hold. I wanted to experience every moment. I became even more willing to look new situations and lessons in the eye and risk the changes that acting on them might bring. I was accepting that there was a loving protector, and I felt safe. As I learned to love myself just as I am, in the perfection of my imperfection, I found less fear. More walls tumbled down. As my perspective changed, so did my choices and my responses. That was difficult for those in my life who were not seeking change for themselves. All I could do at that point was keep the door and my heart open and be respectful of their positions.

Loyalty has always been a defining aspect of my character. As a Leo, born in the Year of the Dog, I don't suppose I can escape it. Perhaps loyalty to others to the detriment of myself was one of the attachments that Patricia had sent me in search of. It was time to be loyal to myself. I made the choice to live alone rather than live with emptiness, and it has been wonder-filled.

Even with understanding and acceptance that our paths were so different, divorce was difficult for me. In reality, it required very little change; the separation was only an acknowledgment of what already was, but I had to give up the dream that we would eventually come together. That was hard. I don't normally quit. There is a place for dogged determination, however, and there is a place for acceptance. It was through acceptance of what was that I was able to move forward.

There were moments of discomfort as we disentangled, each having a purpose and a lesson begging to be noticed. Boundaries were the issue—my boundaries and whether I chose to honor them. I did. I had learned to clearly state what I needed and not to confuse the issue by bringing up the past or worrying about the future. It worked.

Defining needs is quite different than having wants fulfilled. *Wants* are created by the ego and are based in fear. I find that when we want something, we believe that having it will make us more complete. It will fill an empty space or help us to feel better about ourselves. I was wanting nothing. With or without the relationship, I felt complete. I am complete. We all are. There were changes in my life and my perspective, but none diminished the essence of who I am. Nothing can, and knowing that, I knew that there was nothing to fear.

I am so grateful for our years together. I wouldn't wish away one difficult moment, and I cherish the ones when our spirits connected. I learned to distinguish between my ego and the essence of my true being through our interactions. Perhaps the point of our union was for me to do just that. Happily-ever-after may not have been a part of the plan. I am grateful for the teacher—I love the teacher—and I treasure the fruit of our marriage, our four magnificent munchkins. Each a perfect gift at the perfect time, and I always knew that.

The divorce was surprising to most. The kids understood though; they had lived in our home too. They knew where I was coming from, and they celebrated what I was discovering. They wanted us to be happy, and their loving both of us did not require that we reside at the same address. Bless them!

Not everyone else was as generous. Opinions were offered freely. I always listened for the element of truth and then let go of the *what if's*. Others' fears were not something that I needed to concern myself with. Their expectations of me were just that, and I was learning to separate my needs from the needs of others and to be accepting of the differences.

I was asked quite regularly what I was going to do with the rest of my life. I really liked my life and wasn't sure that I was going to do anything very different. I had no plan, and I didn't feel a need to have one. My prayer each morning was for the courage to live the day with an open heart. What doors would open if I did just that?

To simplify the everyday, I began to clean out the closets, the basement, and the patterns and habits that no longer served the direction I was taking. Changes began to occur quite naturally, one of the more significant being that I quit my job as an event coordinator. It had served me beautifully for twelve years. Through the people I worked with and the opportunities presented, I was introduced to new worlds. But the job required that I travel, and I wanted to be at home. Lo and behold, the Universe had a different plan.

Again, I felt a desire to go to the bookstore. I found a copy of *Mastery of Love*, another book authored by Miguel Ruiz. The book has a beautiful message about love and relationships and affirmed much of what I was experiencing. I was intrigued, so much so, that I went to the website printed on the book's cover. That was a miracle in itself, only to be followed by several more. I found a menu and clicked on "teachers." Then I clicked on "Colorado." Of the states listed, it was the closest to my home. The names of two teachers appeared on the screen. They lived in Boulder, and their series of weekend workshops was to begin in two weeks. What really caught my eye, however, was a vision quest they were planning in Wyoming in the spring. I loved being alone outdoors, and the mountains of Wyoming were intriguing. I needed to know nothing more. I reached for the phone. Yes, there were still openings in the class, but I would have to submit a letter of intent to be accepted to the school. Because of their travel schedule, they would be unable to get back to me for ten days. We talked for an hour. It felt to me like the ideal next step, and I hoped that they felt the same.

I wrote the letter, though not being entirely sure what I was supposed to be intent on, and mailed it. I called the airlines. There were seats available. I would have to purchase a ticket before midnight, non-refundable of course, if I wanted a reasonable fare. I did a quick check with my heart. I sensed no fear, so I bought the ticket.

I planned to go to Boulder but didn't get confirmation that I had been admitted to the program until eight o'clock the night before I was to leave. If I could get myself to the Boulderado Hotel by eight the next evening, someone would pick me up. This was a leap of faith, and leap I did. That's one habit that has proved to be worth keeping.

I leapt into the most beautiful place of unconditional love that I could ever have imagined. From the very beginning, there was genuine acceptance. They actually preferred not to know much about us. Our present circumstances mattered not. What brought us to the circle was private if we wished it to be. We simply were enough, in that moment, just as we were.

The group gathered every five weeks for a year. Using time-honored traditions and ceremonies from many cultures, we worked to open our hearts to ourselves and to life. This was a path that I was already traveling, but it was lovely to have the support and camaraderie of community. Many different healing modalities were introduced. We wrote autobiographies beginning with our first memories and working to the present. We also made a list of everyone we had ever met. If there was an emotional reaction to a memory or person, then there was an unresolved issue that needed attention. The work of healing old wounds and forgiveness began there.

We learned to cut cords, attachments that were sapping our energy, and we met our power animals, our spirit guides. We spent hours in the sweat lodge, and we danced and sang and laughed and cried. We began with how we were shaped by past experiences. The intent, however, was for us to move through the old definitions and into the present, a clean slate. We have all allowed ourselves to be defined by labels. Purging those labels was a beautiful adventure.

At some point, one must leave the past in the past and move on. The focus needs to shift from sorting and sifting and fixing to just being. That is what the vision quest in Wyoming was for. It was a time of transition and, I thought, a glorious one. We were in the Big Horn Mountains. After two days of preparation, we each left the base camp in a direction of our own choosing. Being as far from each other as possible was the point. I headed off in the direction of a stream that I could hear. It bubbled and gurgled as the recently melted snow wound over and around the rocks in its path. It was in a hurry to get somewhere. I was enchanted and needed to go no farther. I chose a spot to call home within a grove of young trees and near the water's edge. We had been instructed to create a sacred space by making a circle of corn meal, an ancient tradition, just big enough for ourselves and the few creature comforts we had been allowed to bring along. Mine was about eight feet in diameter. We were also instructed not to leave the circle once it was made. I had with me a sleeping bag and the barest of necessities—an apple, a jug of water, a few nuts, and a new journal.

I was quite alone and in the company of my best friend, myself. I had found her even though she had never been missing, just not seen. I have always loved alone time, possibly because of the scarcity of it, but on that mountaintop, I was able to clearly see the difference between *alone* and *lonely*. My space was filled to overflowing.

The neighborhood squirrels and birds were curious and visited frequently. They were intrigued with the cornmeal. They looked at it and touched it several times, but they didn't eat it or walk on it. They too honored the sacred boundaries. As I watched the squirrels, I thought about how animals serve as spirit guides. Squirrels are masters of preparation. I wondered what I might be preparing for.

I experienced complete joy and gratitude as I rested in the beauty and peace of the mountain. I watched the sun as it moved across the sky and listened to the stream. I saw the auras of the trees and leaves overhead and fell asleep under the magnificence of starlit heavens. I framed thoughts as little as possible. When they came, I wrote them down for later consideration. I could easily have stayed for days, but the plans only allowed for thirty hours.

When we came off the mountain, I was in a state of total bliss. I really knew for sure that what I needed in this lifetime I already had. I always had had it, but now I knew it. I wanted to wrap myself around that moment so that I wouldn't forget, but I didn't have to. Parked at the base of the mountain, sixty miles from the nearest town, smack dab in the middle of nowhere, was a big, beautiful, orange eighteen-wheeler, and the last thing that I would ever have expected to see at that moment. Life has such a wonderful sense of humor! Now I am adding "you're enough" to the "you're okay" message.

I don't tend to be a very regimented person. Incorporating what I have learned into the day-to-day often requires ritual, and I don't do that very well. I attended classes on mindfulness, taught in the Buddhist tradition, as an another way to bring focus to the present and to eliminate the constant chatter of the mind. Did it really serve me to multitask, watch the news on TV, have music on in the background, or read while I was eating? It was a question without right or wrong answers but one worth exploring. We used meditation and yoga to center ourselves and to explore the intentions of our actions. These classes added great awareness to the significance of the seemingly insignificant choices I was making. They helped me to understand how making different choices would quiet the mind and support peace of mind. Again, it was a message that I had heard many times and simply needed to practice. It required living in consciousness to let go of the old and make space for the new.

I have referred to what I have "learned" many times, but more accurately, I want to say that the many avenues I have explored have helped me to remember. When something rings true, it has the sense of the familiar, not a feeling of newness. I have heard others say the same. As a ninth grader, algebra felt like new information, but discovering a truth has been like finding an old friend.

I believe that there is danger in being a perpetual student and thinking that someone else has the answers for us; no one else does. Collective wisdom has served beautifully by providing signposts on the path, but at some point, one must trust that all that is needed is found in the simplicity of one's being. It is through remembering that I have found the wings to soar and the desire to just let go.

Walking through
the Open Door

a year came and went very quickly. Each day was amazing and full of promise, often without routine and predictability. Some friendships changed, as did many of the "normal" activities, but there were no voids, only spaces created to embrace the new and different that ventured in—sometimes so quietly that I hardly noticed. Everything I did, I did because I chose to do it.

For several years I have volunteered at a local elementary school. I tutor the students with all the labels that usually add up to failure. Each little scamp steals my heart, typically within the first five minutes of our meeting.

I have a distinct advantage over a classroom teacher. I work one on one. That way it is easier to keep the kids focused, and I can adapt to individual learning styles when I can figure them out. They learn fast, and there can be fear associated with that because it is unfamiliar. They are used to not measuring up. It has become part of their identity to fail. I am such a master of resistance that I understand them completely. We are a perfect match.

This year, I was given the rascal of all rascals to tutor. He was a first grade whirling dervish with a heart of gold. The first time I met him, his head was on the floor, and his feet were kicking in the air as his tummy straddled his desk chair. He was yelling at another child across the room. It was the second week of school, and so far this was normal. He had spent a significant amount of time in the office because the staff had not been able to identify a way to grab his attention; his disruptive behavior was unfair to the other students in the class. He was incorrigible and utterly adorable—all at the same time.

We normally worked together for an hour each day. Darius struggled for months to learn letters and their sounds. He really tried, but his progress was slow. What words he could read were memorized, a beginning. The world of phonics was a complete mystery. School, in the traditional manner, did not make sense to this child.

For Christmas I bought him the book *Go, Dog! Go*. It is an easy reader that was way too difficult for him, but it was the best that the bookstore could do. He brought the book to school after the holidays. Could I teach him to read it? "Absolutely," I said, wondering how that was going to happen. We read the first ten pages over and over. He struggled, but he kept trying. Then suddenly, and for no apparent reason, something started to click, and he began to sound out the words. We were both astonished.

One morning he asked what we would read when we finished "Go, Dog." I was impressed by his hopefulness and told him that I would be happy to buy him another book. "And after that?" I said I would buy him another. I told him that I would buy an entire library for him if need be.

He worked hard—even practicing at home after school. By mid March he had read seven books. Our next and greatest challenge was *Green Eggs and Ham*, a personal favorite of mine. Again, we read the first few pages over and over until he had a sense of comfort. He was feeling wonderfully confident until we arrived at a page that had about sixty words on it. It was a simple recap of earlier pages, but it looked ominous. He groaned and put his head down on the table. He was sure he couldn't read it, and I assured him that I knew he could. I suggested he take a little rest and rubbed his back while he moaned and groaned. Finally, he took a deep breath and sat up. He thought he was ready to begin. I was just loving the drama he was creating. With great trepidation, he read the first word and the second. One by one he tackled each word on the page, never faltering. By the time he got to the last one, he was grinning from ear to ear. I asked him what he was feeling. He didn't want to tell me. I asked him again. To me, the important part of our work together was self-discovery, and I took every opportunity presented to assist him in this arena. This seemed like a good one, and I wasn't willing to let it pass. After a long pause he said very quietly, "I love Darius Jones," referring to himself. He then proceeded to read the last forty pages of the book. He stood up, gave me a hug, picked up the book, and walked to class as if nothing out of the ordinary had happened. I just sat in my chair, dumbfounded, with tears welling in my eyes.

His classroom teacher was gone for the day, so I shared the story with the principal. As I was leaving her office, I shouted, "I love Darius Jones." Very quietly she said, "That sounds like the title of a book."

I bounced all the way home and into the next day. I had a new book for my little buddy, and he sailed through it. He was nothing less than amazing. After school I went to the bookstore to find another addition for his growing library. Shortly after getting home, it started to snow. The snow was falling so heavily it seemed like it might never stop. The huge wet flakes were sticking to everything in their path—creating a peaceful white blanket. It was enchantingly beautiful and serene. As I watched from the warmth of my family room, a rhyme started going through my head. It was about my little friend. I wrote down what I was hearing and in a couple of hours had a wonderful little story before me. It was about his transition from a frustrated troublemaker to a child who loved himself. As I reread it, I noticed that it was written in his reading vocabulary. Of course the title had to be *I Love Darius Jones*.

School was canceled the next day because of the deep snow, so I went to the computer and started creating pages. I made words in big type and little type and even one that slumped, just like his schoolwork. This is possibly the most amazing part of the story. I have never wanted to take the time needed to develop a relationship with the world of technology, and my literacy usually reflects just that, but not on that day.

The next day, I showed him "his" book and asked if he would like to illustrate it. He was very uncomfortable and quite reluctant. He didn't know if he liked it. It took three days to discover why he was hesitant. He finally asked me, "Is it okay to say you love yourself?" Well, if it hadn't been before, it certainly was now! We showed the book to his teacher, and her enthusiasm helped him over the hump. We worked on the drawings for a couple of weeks. He shared his book with every staff member and class that would listen. The entire school supported his discovery of self-love. He was even given the opportunity to read it to the president of St. Paul Companies, Inc., a local insurance company. His performance was magical. He was the most endearing child that one might imagine, and I will always remember the beautiful smile on his face when he read the title to his esteemed audience. It was a moment of perfection.

The next day I felt jubilant as I walked into school. What would today bring? It brought the news that my special buddy was moving and would be transferring schools immediately. Timing is everything. I can only imagine how much help we were getting behind the scenes as we scurried to complete our work together. It was obvious to me that we had been lovingly guided all along. The magnificence of life just unfolded—effortlessly. All my little friend and I needed to do was show up, and we did that regularly.

I waited a couple of weeks before going to visit my little friend in his new school. He has had a tough time adjusting. The staff has helped as best they can. They, too, see that beautiful heart. He keeps his library in his backpack so that, at a moment's notice, he can read to a willing ear. He reported to me that his favorite book is the one we wrote, and that's now my favorite too.

I was tempted to leave the school where we met and the other children that I tutor and join him in his new school. I finally decided against it. I think our work together is done. We each learned many things that changed our lives. Now it is our job to move forward, each with a new perspective.

This love story is all about being open to possibilities. Who would have thought that this feisty little boy who got kicked off the school bus on a regular basis for fighting would discover the power of self-love? Who would have thought that he would be reading avidly in such a short time and place such value in having a library of his own? Who would have thought that his story would be written down and printed out on my computer? Certainly not I!

Our little journey together is a microcosmic example of a

journey through life—taking baby steps and building on the past experiences little by little but not allowing them to define us. He is so much more than what he has done in his short life. As in all of us, the God within is just bursting to shine in that precious child. He now knows that it is there, and I trust there is a special reason for that. How fortunate I was to have walked by his side, if only for a short while. He took me to magical places, and it was so easy. We held hands, began with something familiar, had a sense of where we wanted to go, and took the first step. The rest was in God's hands, and look where we ended up! I think it helped that we laughed a lot along the way.

This is not an uncommon story. I had the opportunity to hear Helen Prejean, the nun who wrote *Dead Man Walking*, speak this spring. What a fascinating woman and a passionate, loving speaker she is. Her sense of humor is bright and lively, and the audience was instantly engaged. She spoke first of how sneaky God is. Just when you are least expecting it, He nudges very gently. You aren't even aware of His presence until suddenly you are in a place that you never would have chosen on your own. Opportunity and growth await when we are able to recognize that the Divine is present. We can choose fear and back away, or we can choose to rest in the safety of the Almighty's arms and continue on. I have found myself in the same situation so many times that I knew of what she spoke.

She told of how she was asked to be a pen pal for an inmate on death row. It seemed like a simple request at first blush, but it led her down an unfamiliar road and to the primary focus of her life's work. Her pen pal was a young man who had participated in a heinous crime, the rape and murder of a teenager and her boyfriend. She connected with his spirit and loved him as a child of God, as we all are, long before she learned the nature of his crime. That changed nothing. She knew him as someone far greater than his actions and saw the beauty of the soul within. She is quite remarkable.

At the same time, she also chose to be sympathetic and loving to the families of his victims. Each had a place in the story. Each was suffering. She did not take sides. Helen's gift was unconditional love and support for all involved. In a situation filled with hatred and outrage, she chose love over vengeance and walked beside a con-victed murderer as his spiritual guide and friend when he was led to his death. Her gentle love for this fellow human being stilled the audience. I know we each left that evening wondering how we could add our own version of gentle love to the equation. What kind of world would we create if we did?

Helen Prejean's story and her work for Amnesty International are fascinating to me. I see a connection between her story, my little darlings at school, and my adorable pup. I believe the overriding issue is safety. Physical safety has not been a teacher for me in this lifetime—except through others. Mine has ne

ened, but I see it as an important component

standing of others.

Safety is a basic need for survival in this worl

ing aware of the effects that the lack thereof prod

has been a notable teacher. I adopted him at the

golden retriever rescue group; he had a very prec

He was treated for malnourishment at two mont

cued from his unhealthy surroundings by a veter

eventually placed in a loving home. They spent a y

answers to the incontinence that plagued him an

family. When there seemed to be little hope of find

tion or a solution for the condition, they placed hi

cue group. They felt they could no longer keep him,

beautiful spirit they did not want to put him down.

Lucky and I met on the Internet. He was the "f

month" on the rescue group's website. He had been th

several months. No one wanted him. I didn't want h

was looking for a low maintenance companion, older

able, and healthy was a must. There were several dogs

to be good candidates, but they were adopted by familie

the waiting list than I. My turn would come.

She told of how she was asked to be a pen pal for an inmate on death row. It seemed like a simple request at first blush, but it led her down an unfamiliar road and to the primary focus of her life's work. Her pen pal was a young man who had participated in a heinous crime, the rape and murder of a teenager and her boyfriend. She connected with his spirit and loved him as a child of God, as we all are, long before she learned the nature of his crime. That changed nothing. She knew him as someone far greater than his actions and saw the beauty of the soul within. She is quite remarkable.

At the same time, she also chose to be sympathetic and loving to the families of his victims. Each had a place in the story. Each was suffering. She did not take sides. Helen's gift was unconditional love and support for all involved. In a situation filled with hatred and outrage, she chose love over vengeance and walked beside a convicted murderer as his spiritual guide and friend when he was led to his death. Her gentle love for this fellow human being stilled the audience. I know we each left that evening wondering how we could add our own version of gentle love to the equation. What kind of world would we create if we did?

Helen Prejean's story and her work for Amnesty International are fascinating to me. I see a connection between her story, my little darlings at school, and my adorable pup. I believe the overriding issue is safety. Physical safety has not been a teacher for me in this lifetime—except through others. Mine has never truly been threatened, but I see it as an important component when seeking understanding of others.

Safety is a basic need for survival in this world. I am fast becoming aware of the effects that the lack thereof produces. Again, Lucky has been a notable teacher. I adopted him at the age of two from a golden retriever rescue group; he had a very precarious beginning. He was treated for malnourishment at two months of age and rescued from his unhealthy surroundings by a veterinarian. He was eventually placed in a loving home. They spent a year trying to find answers to the incontinence that plagued him and frustrated his family. When there seemed to be little hope of finding an explanation or a solution for the condition, they placed him with the rescue group. They felt they could no longer keep him, and seeing his beautiful spirit they did not want to put him down.

Lucky and I met on the Internet. He was the "feature of the month" on the rescue group's website. He had been the feature for several months. No one wanted him. I didn't want him either. I was looking for a low maintenance companion, older was preferable, and healthy was a must. There were several dogs that looked to be good candidates, but they were adopted by families higher on the waiting list than I. My turn would come.

Early one morning my veterinarian called. He knew that I was looking for a dog, and he had heard of a golden retriever breeder with a puppy. He encouraged me to call her immediately, and I did. Yes, she had one puppy left, but she thought she wanted to keep him. He was the pick of the litter and a good candidate for the show ring. She wanted two more weeks to monitor his physical development, and then she would decide. We had several interesting conversations about dogs and life while we waited for the pup to grow. I really liked her. When she decided to keep Dakota, I wasn't disappointed; I had learned many things from her. Perhaps that was the purpose for our connection.

I told her that I had enjoyed our many conversations and that I knew that the perfect dog would come along. I mentioned that I was on the waiting list for a rescue dog, and to make a long story short, she was Lucky's foster mom, and he was at her feet as we were speaking. Her adoring description of him didn't soften my will. I had no desire to adopt an incontinent dog.

I did, however, offer to do energy healings so that his situation might be remedied and a permanent home found. She accepted the offer readily. She had been using a variety of holistic treatments to improve his condition. Acupuncture and an organic diet with supplements seemed to be helping. The energy work did as well.

Lucky seemed to be on the road to recovery, and I am a sucker for amber eyes and a tail that is so enthusiastic it wags the whole dog. You know the rest of the story.

Lucky was not in our home for more than a couple of hours before his history started to reveal itself. He had an extreme fear of tall men, particularly tall men with intense dispositions. He snarled and lunged viciously when they came to the door or to the garden gate, but he was easily calmed by my assurances that they were okay. I checked with his foster mom. She had noticed the same behavior as well, but he had little exposure to other people in the eight months he lived at her kennel, and she had forgotten about it. His behavior seemed rather odd, but he was in a strange place with strange people and had been several times. It seemed that he had a right to keep his guard up. I learned to be very careful with him.

One afternoon, I got the broom to sweep the back porch, one of his favorite haunts. When he saw me coming he ran to the far corner of the yard and peeked out from behind a tree. I thought he looked quite cute until I noticed that he was shaking with fear. Somewhere along the line, Lucky had obviously had a bad experience with a broom. I am guessing that it also may have involved a tall man with an intense demeanor. Lucky hadn't felt safe at some point in his short life, and he had the physical and emotional behaviors to prove it.

It took two years for Lucky to have faith in me, the same amount of time that he had lived apart from me. If he were going to make an investment in our relationship, I was going to have to prove myself worthy. Apparently I did because with nothing else being different, he suddenly began to sit when asked, come when I called, and relax into what I would call a normal routine. The dribbling began to subside as well, though that has mattered less as I have perfected the art of dog diapering. What a patient boy he has been! I am now on my way to having an older, low maintenance, healthy dog. It all started with a nudge by a very sneaky God.

What Lucky needed was to be accepted—just as he was. That acceptance created the space for him to begin to heal. He has come so far; if there is more for him to do, he will do it. He isn't a quitter, just like someone else I know and love. What a magnificent teacher and companion he has been. I love his spirit.

I love the spirits of my kids at school, too, and they can be so out of control sometimes that I don't really want to be in their presence. Helen Prejean believed her pen pal had a beautiful spirit as well. I am guessing that her pen pal and my students also have had issues with safety. When they act out, I am also going to guess that it is due to fear, and we can choose to treat them with love and compassion or deliver more pain in the form of judgment and condemnation. It is difficult to respond to fear with love, particularly if the fear is displayed with violence, but I think that we should try.

I believe that violence comes not from evil but from pain. Lucky isn't evil, and my bouncing-off-the-wall first grader isn't evil, but if we choose to ignore their pain, they could become dangerous like the young man on death row. When we see each other as we wish to be seen, then we can create a world that is safe for all. Helen Prejean has made that choice. The rest of us can too.

Always Enough

$\mathcal{S}pring$ break was approaching, and I decided that I was going to take a road trip. I selected the Grand Canyon as my destination, and my friend Darcie decided to come along for the ride. Having no particular plan, we drove off in the general direction of Arizona. We were just going to let the spirit move us, and it did. We found ourselves in some very interesting situations, and as always, with excellent teachers nearby.

The many hours in the car gave us plenty of opportunity to explore our current situations in life. My traveling companion was struggling with ghosts of the past. I listened intently and was able to see glimpses of my journey that ran parallel to hers. When Darcie would recognize a place where she felt stuck or discouraged, I would hear myself offering gentle questions. Is that love or fear? How does that pattern serve you? Do you really believe that, or is that the opinion of another? Each question was perfect. We both knew they were not coming from me, but through me, and they were being asked for my benefit as well as hers. She was able to clarify some of her walls and boundaries, as was I. She was grateful for the questions, and I was thankful for her presence and for seeing the reflection of my journey through hers. It was a perfect flow of giving and receiving. Though the experience was different for us both, as we are different from each other, we each gained what was needed.

Our adventures were hilarious. There is one in particular that stands out as life altering for me. We arrived in Flagstaff at dusk one evening desperately needing food and a place to sleep. We drove down a main street searching for both when I noticed that the palms of my hands were itching. We weren't finding what we needed on our own, so just for fun, we decided to venture into the unknown and let the energy in my hands direct us.

I turned right when my right palm itched and left when the left palm itched. We had a grand tour of Flagstaff, laughing all the way. Within about fifteen minutes, we found ourselves right back where we had started, still without food and a place to stop for the night. There was a motel on the corner. We had noticed it the first time around, but it looked full, and it turned out that it was. They recommended one down the street, around the bend, under the railroad tracks, and a few blocks farther on the right. We followed the directions. Both my hands were itching like crazy, but we kept our focus toward the right, watching for the motel that would bring an end to this day's journey.

As we emerged from under the railroad bridge, our attention was focused to the right, but we both spotted a simply lit sign on the left side of the street, "Palm Reader, $10." We had to go! The motel was located directly across the street. We pulled into the parking lot, registered for a room as fast as we could, ran across six lanes of traffic to the palm reader's door, and rang the bell.

The door opened slowly, and a soft voice invited us to enter. We saw no one and were a bit hesitant. A woman then quietly moved from behind the door into our field of vision. She was dressed in black; her hair was dyed to match. Her eyes were deeply set and ringed with dark circles. Her manner was gentle, and she had an air of mystery. We would have expected nothing less. We started to explain why we had come. I held up my hands and began to tell her about my itchy palms only to discover that it was no longer so. We had found the place where we were supposed to be.

I found Judy's reading to be very accurate regarding past experiences and the purposes thereof. For the future, she saw me moving and writing a book. I told her I had just written the story of my little friend. No, that wasn't it. She said I was to write about my spiritual journey and advised me to begin immediately.

What a preposterous idea! I had no desire to write a book. I had never even considered the possibility of writing one. Just to humor her, I asked how I was to begin. She didn't know and said, "You will find your way." She was making the assumption that I would try. I didn't want to tell her that she might be mistaken.

As I waited in the quiet of the outer room while Darcie was having her palms read, I began to remember the many times someone had suggested I write down my stories. I started to sweat. I didn't believe that there would be value in writing about my experiences.

Was this something worth considering, a door opening? I truly doubted it; it felt like total foolishness to me.

We shared our readings while eating dinner. I reluctantly told Darcie the part about the book. My sweet companion then took it upon herself to explain the many reasons why I should write one. She talked at me until three a.m. I begged for mercy, but there was none until I agreed to try. "Just start writing," she said over and over again. I didn't believe it was going to be that easy, but I awoke later that morning with the introductory story of Lucky running through my head. "I think I know how the book is to begin," I said in response to her cheerful "Good morning."

The rest of the trip was equally enchanting. The Grand Canyon is so spectacular! We were there during the full moon, a time of abundance, and indeed the entire adventure had been. We arrived home with a better sense of our being and new directions for our lives. The Universe had showered us with blessings. I couldn't stop grinning for a week.

It also took a week for me to take pencil and paper in hand and begin my new project. I felt totally ill prepared and inadequate for the job, so I called on my angels and asked for guidance. They came, and they gave. The words also came, with ease, making this a thoroughly enjoyable adventure.

As to the value of my musings, I can say that it has been

exceptional for me. That alone makes it worthy. Hindsight has been a useful tool in seeing the opportunities lovingly presented by the grace of our ever-present, all-powerful God. My wake-up call, Susan's death, was sudden and painful. I think wake-up calls usually are. Was Susan's passing the only way for me to begin acknowledging the spirit within and around me? No, I don't believe so, but her passing was an opportunity to do so. She was completing her own circle of life, regardless of my presence. The opportunity to walk side by side for a bit was a gift, God's love incarnate. Her passing was as well if I chose to see it that way, and fortunately, after the first jolt, I did. Too much had led us to that moment together for me to believe that her physical death was only an ending. It became the most beautiful of beginnings for me and, I trust, for her as well.

It took my believing that something beautiful had ended for the real work to begin—the sorting of emotions, ailments, and the relationships with myself, to the people in my midst and the God within. Quite possibly, it could have been a frightening journey if not taken one step at a time: watching, listening, taking a deep breath, sometimes looking for a hand to hold, and then proceeding into the unknown. I was never alone, and I have never been alone, although it sometimes felt that I was. There has never been anything to fear but the *what if*'s that I put in the middle of the road. The changes were many, but none proved to be as difficult as living with the fear and feelings of inadequacy I had been hiding behind for so many years.

Freedom is possible. It comes through the willingness to recognize the spirit that lives in us, to allow that spirit to move through us, and to let our hearts sing. The ego has to go. Brian Andreas has written a story, *Illusion of Control*. Incorporated within it is a line drawing of a very whimsical woman sitting in an overturned umbrella. Her story is, " 'If you hold on to the handle,' she said, 'it's easier to maintain the illusion of control. But it's more fun if you just let the wind carry you.' " She is on to something.

I have sometimes ignored and dismissed and been resistant to the love that is within us and around us. Lacking understanding, or a sense of purpose, I have been discouraged and frustrated. But, even when I wanted to throw in the proverbial towel, I couldn't. I couldn't quit, and life never quit on me either. The love of God is limitless, forgiving, and ever present, and the perfect opportunity for realizing that is presented at the perfect time, in the perfect way, and by the perfect teacher.

I have noticed a big difference in the teachers that now show up at my door. As I have learned to live with a more compassionate, open heart, the teachers have presented themselves in a more compassionate, loving way. The mirror now has a loving reflection. Life is gentle and joyful and totally amazing each blessed day.

I do not always live in that place of acceptance and peace, but I do my best. The difference I see now is that when I feel fearful and unloving, I don't stay there for very long. I know to look for the source of the discomfort within, within me. There, too, is where peace resides.

Just recently, I was in Los Angeles for ten days. I was given an opportunity to see how much I missed my old job. I don't. I was willing to fill in temporarily because it gave me an opportunity to visit my son and his bride in their new home. After working for a week in complete chaos, which is thankfully no longer the norm in my life, I needed a nature fix. My California dreamer took me to the Getty Center to wander the massive grounds and gardens. We found a bronze plaque planted in a pathway. It reads:

Ever present,
Never twice the same,
Ever changing,
Never less than whole.

That says it all. As we move through this lifetime, no matter what we are doing, where we are, or whom we are with, we are complete. Everything that we need for this journey is already a part of us, within us. There is no need to question and no reason to doubt that. We are always, and ever, enough.

———— ⋅⊗⋅ ————

There Is

a

Purpose

———— ⋅⊗⋅ ————

have found a new definition for who I am. I am not the story, or the events, or the roles I have played in this lifetime. I have merely used, and am still using, them to uncover the essence of my being, to touch the God within. Everything in my life has been purposeful and has served to teach or guide me to go within. I have found many of the greatest teachers to be in the smallest of things: a smile, a feeling, a flock of geese flying overhead, a weed, a caustic comment, or a choice, maybe one that is so obscure that I don't even realize I am making it. Whatever is before us teaches.

I am so very thankful for each bump in the road, each teacher presented, and each new day. Each has provided me with the opportunity to learn about love if I so choose, and I am now choosing to do just that. I am choosing to see the presence of God in all things. I believe that everyone and everything contains the element of goodness—the life force that flows through us and connects us to all things and each other.

I can't say that I have found the answers. I haven't. What I have done is find joy in living with the questions. Each has offered an opportunity to relinquish my hold on the familiar and walk in uncharted territory. Each has been an avenue for gaining new insight and understanding. Each has had purpose. I now see the God within us all, and I believe in the magnificence of our very being. We *are* one. We are one with the Universe and one with each other. Could there be a greater purpose for our lives than to discover just that? I don't have the answer, but I am willing to embrace the question and see where it takes me.

Acknowledgments

I do not see myself as an author. I will admit, however, to creating the space for the words to come in their own time and place. This grand adventure has had very little to do with writing—it has been a wonder-filled lesson in listening. I am intrigued by the end result and grateful for the guidance offered by Archangel Michael. His radiant blue light is ever present.

I am eternally thankful for my beautiful family and the friends who encouraged me to begin sifting and sorting through the pieces of the puzzle. Thankfully, Darcie Grim was relentless. "Just write," she said over and over again as I offered excuses to ignore the suggestion that I do so. The only way to quiet her was to try.

Ann Geery, Pat McGuigan, and Marna Morgan had the courage to read the first draft. Their gentle questions, loving observations, and encouragement led me to believe that *Not Afraid...* had a life with purpose. I discovered the direction that this book wished to take when working with Phyllis Lahn, in New York, last spring. She mentioned that she had a friend living in Minneapolis who had just published a book. She gave me Judie White's phone number and suggested that I call. I did. I was pleasantly surprised to find that Judie had self-published, and she generously offered advice and the names of her suppliers. As she spoke of the importance of a graphic designer, the name of Cory Barton popped into my head. Cory is a family friend. We had not seen much of each other for years but had reason to meet a few weeks prior to my conversation with Judie. At that time I asked Cory about her graphic design business. It was going well; she had developed a base of clients who embraced her passion, gardening and flowers. I called Cory to see if dandelions would fall into either category, and she enthusiastically agreed to join me on this adventure.

And so it goes, the right person, with the right information, and the right talent, at the right time.

My editors have been patient and kind. Each has contributed endless hours to the cause. Betsy Fabel was sweet and gentle as she encouraged me to let the adjectives flow and the images take shape. Joanne Fabel offered undying enthusiasm and support. She loves rules and showed me how to bring clarity with a recognizable sentence structure. And another tenacious Patricia, Patricia Whiteford, sat by my side for days and, with her sense of humor ever present, insisted that I *use* a recognizable sentence structure.

Jeanne Steele, a long-time friend, needed a project for her

marketing class at the University of St.Thomas. She asked if I would be willing to let them develop a marketing plan for *Not Afraid*.... What a gift! The class was delightful and resourceful and they presented three well-executed final projects for my consideration. One of the many contributions is the copy on the dust jacket.

Jim Bindas, of Book Productions, LLC, has coordinated the printing process. He returns phone calls immediately and does exactly what he says he will do. It has been a pleasure to work with him.

I am grateful to Barbara Kingsolver and Brian Andreas, the creator of StoryPeople, for graciously allowing me to directly quote their works. Some things are better left just as they are. I treasure the wisdom of both authors.

For all who have shared some part of themselves with me, I offer my love and gratitude. I have been blessed by your presence. May peace be with you always.

To order *Not Afraid to Live with Dandelions* please contact:
La Pointe Press
P O Box 16063 Elway Station
St. Paul, MN 55116
651.238.4567